Twenty Five Favou
West Surrey ar

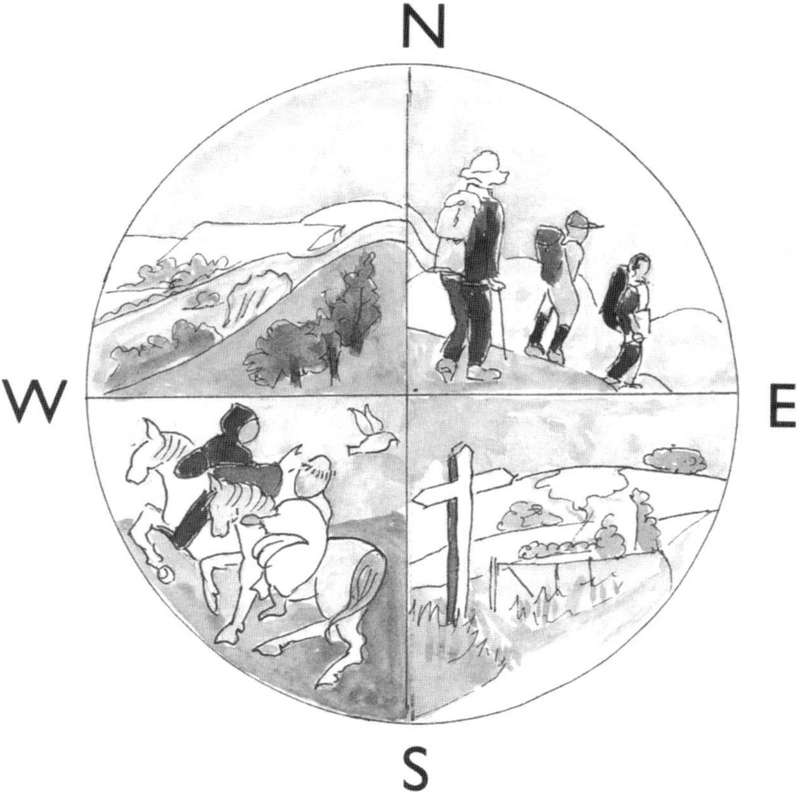

A revised edition of 'Favourite Walks' compiled by members of the
Godalming and Haslemere Group of the Ramblers' Association and now offering
25 circular walks from $2^1/2$ - $16^1/4$ miles ranging from the North Downs in Surrey to the
South Downs in Sussex.

With many of the walks offering longer and shorter versions a total of 45 different options
are described.

Map showing distribution of walks

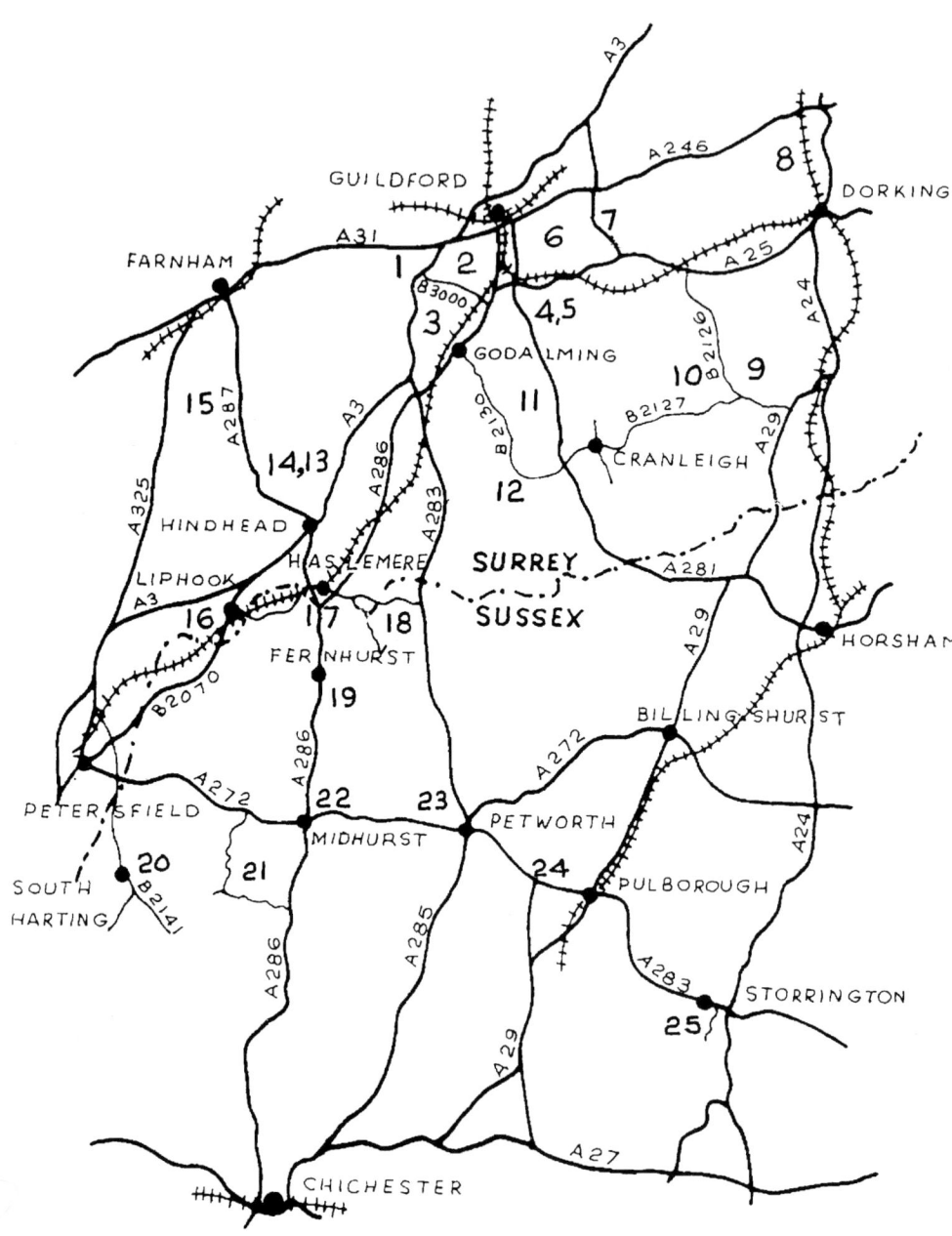

The numbers indicate the starting points of the walks.

Contents

		Miles	Page
	Notes for users		5
1	Cutmill Ponds - Puttenham Common *Damian and Elizabeths' walk*	6 or 3^1/$_2$	6
2	Compton - Loseley Park *Michael's walk*	5^1/$_2$ or 6	8
3	Godalming - North Downs Way - River Wey *Eric and Hazel's walk*	11	10
4	Blackheath - Pitch Hill - Farley Green *George and Mary's walk*	9	12
5	Blackheath - Smithwood Common - Shamley Green *William's walk*	12^1/$_2$	15
6	Newlands Corner - Tilling Bourne Valley *Roger and Margaret's walk*	6^3/$_4$ or 7^1/$_2$	18
7	Abinger Roughs - Abinger Common - Wotton *Audrey's walk*	5^3/$_4$ or 6	20
8	Ranmore - North Downs Way - Polesden Lacey *John and Joyce's walk*	6^3/$_4$	23
9	Holmwood Common - Coldharbour - Leith Hill *Olga's walk*	10 or 2^1/$_2$ or 7^1/$_2$	25
10	Friday Street - Leith Hill - Abinger Common *John and Joyce's walk*	9 or 6^1/$_2$ or 13^1/$_2$	28
11	Hydon Heath - Hambledon - Hascombe *Jean's walk*	9 or 8	30
12	Dunsfold - Sussex Border Path - Plaistow *Julian's walk*	9^1/$_4$	32
13	Hindhead - Hammer - Waggoners Wells *Joy's walk*	12^1/$_2$	36

14	Hindhead - Thursley - Hankley Common *Norman and Jeverley's walk*	10 or 12	40
15	Frensham Ponds - Shortfield Common *Denis and Susan's walk*	$10^{1}/_{2}$ or 6 or $4^{1}/_{2}$	43
16	Liphook - Milland - Wardley Moor *Barrie and Margaret's walk*	11 or 5	47
17	Haslemere - Chiddingfold - Frillinghurst *Richard's walk*	$9^{1}/_{2}$	50
18	Blackdown - Henley - Fernhurst *John and Christine's walk*	12	53
19	Fernhurst - Lurgashall - Northchapel *Lionel's walk*	$9^{1}/_{4}$ or 4 or $5^{1}/_{2}$	56
20	Harting Down - South Downs Way - Compton *Sybil's walk*	8	58
21	Didling - Cocking - South Downs Way *Ernst and Ursula's walk*	10	60
22	Midhurst - Lodsworth - Easebourne *Jessie's walk*	9 or 7	62
23	Petworth Park - Lurgashall - River Common *John and Christine's walk*	12 or 10 or 6	66
24	Fittleworth - Burton Mill - Bedham - Stopham *Monica's walk*	$16^{1}/_{4}$ or 7 or $9^{1}/_{4}$	69
25	Chantry Post - South Downs Way - Findon *Roger and Jill's walk*	$11^{3}/_{4}$	76

British Library Cataloguing in Publication Data. A catalogue record for this book is available from the British Library.

ISBN 1-901184-16-1

First published as *'21 Favourite Walks in Surrey and Sussex'* 1995 and reprinted May 1996. This fully revised and expanded edition, *'25 Favourite Walks in West Surrey and Sussex'* published April 1999.

© Godalming and Haslemere Ramblers' Association Group.

Copies of this book obtainable by post [add 50p postage please] from Rosemary Bryant, Kinfauns Cottage, Petworth Road, Witley, Surrey GU8 5QW.

Notes for Users

All walks are circular and except for the shorter ones, are often planned to include a pub-stop around the half-way stage, while favourite picnic spots are often mentioned. However, do check the sketch map for the position along the route of a pub or refreshment spot and plan accordingly: for example in one case [walk 5] a pub which for many years provided a break mid-way round has recently closed so a picnic is now a good idea! The information at the start of each walk includes all the pub and refreshment stops on the route or close by and does not imply any particular recommendation.

The maps referred to are the Ordnance Survey [OS] Landranger series 1:50,000 [$1^1/_4$ ins. to 1 mile] and the new Explorer series 1:25,000 [$2^1/_2$ ins. to 1 mile]. Both show Public Rights of Way. The Explorer series is designed for walkers and includes field boundaries and other detail which is helpful. An OS Grid Reference [GR] is given to locate the start of each walk and applies to either map. Instructions for using these are on the maps but briefly, the first two figures refer to the numbered grid lines at the top/bottom of the sheet, while the third figure is an estimation in tenths of the distance from it to the desired point. The final three figures refer similarly to the grid numbers down the sides. While information is given to help you find the start of each walk we recommend that you refer to the relevant OS map.

The numbers in the walk descriptions relate to those on the sketch maps and we have aimed to make the two together sufficient for you to find your way. However it is always best to have a map handy and an excellent way to become familiar with using an OS map is to relate the sketches and description to the information on the map as you go. You can then vary the walks as you wish and continue to explore our rich heritage of paths for yourself, finding your own favourites. On heaths and commons in particular, a compass is also useful to check your direction.

Possible public transport links are outlined but as bus services and even bus routes are now very changeable the only reliable advice is to ring one of the following numbers for up to date information on services offered by any of the bus companies. They also send leaflets on request.

Surrey Travel Line	01737 223000
Sussex Travel Line	0345 959099
Rail services	0345 484950

The following abbreviations are used: N [North], S [South], E [East], W [West], OS [Ordnance Survey], trig point [OS triangulation pillar], NT [National Trust], GR [OS Grid Reference], PH or pub [Public House], CP [car park]. Others are explained in the text.

The routes described use public Rights of Way except in some areas managed by the Forestry Commission, National Trust or Hurtwood Control, where public use of paths is permitted [permissive paths]. Over time some paths may be legally diverted or extinguished, so please remember that small changes of route may become necessary. These should be clearly signed by the County Council. Obstructions to Rights of Way should be reported to the Ramblers' Association Central Office, 1/5 Wandsworth Road, London SW8 who will inform the appropriate local representative.

1 Cutmill Ponds – North Downs Way – Puttenham Common

Damian and Elizabeth's walk

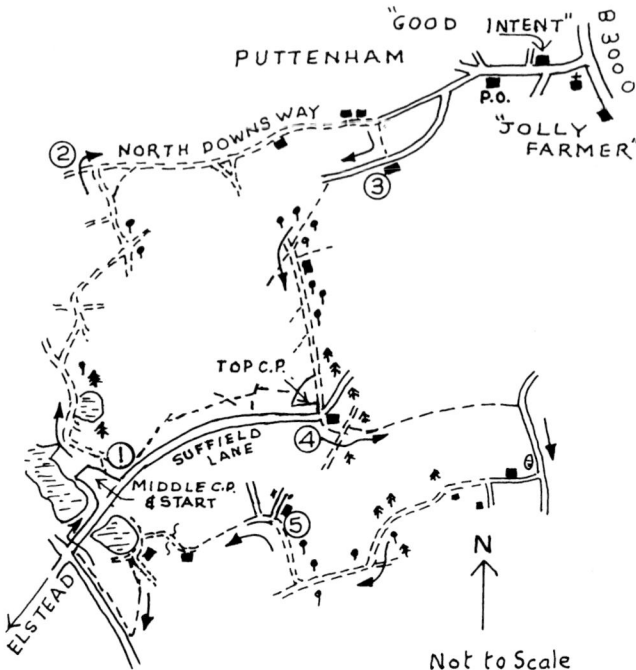

Length: 6 miles plus two shorter versions of 3 1/2 miles: version A [omit 1,2&3] or version B [omit 4&5].

Maps: OS Landranger 186; Explorer 145

Start: GR 912457 Middle Car Park, Puttenham Common, [near Cutmill Pond], on minor road, Suffield Lane, between Puttenham and Elstead.

Transport: Tillingbourne buses Godalming - Farnham and Guildford, to the Post Office, Puttenham and walk 1/2 mile to join at 3 [see map].

Refreshments: The Good Intent PH and The Jolly Farmer, 'Harvester' pub in Puttenham [see map].

Introduction: The walk is varied, passing through heathland, farmland and wooded areas, and is generally well drained. There are some fine views particularly from the Upper Puttenham Common Car Park.

THE WALK

Shorter version A. Take the pathways going uphill towards the Puttenham Common Top Car Park. These run for 1/2 mile with Suffield Lane nearby on your right. When you reach the Top Car Park follow the driveway down to the minor road, Suffield Lane, and continue with sections 4 and 5 of the walk.

Full version and shorter version B.
1. Begin the walk by taking the path just to the left of the information board and follow the mauve nature trail direction posts. After a few yards ignore a pathway on the left and carry on through trees, passing four more nature trail posts. On reaching a wide track turn right, keeping straight on over wooden sleepers and veering left with General's Pond on your right. After about a quarter of a mile take a right fork by an indicator post, following the sandy track up the hill. Near the top of the hill, just past another indicator post, take the left branch at a fork with an indicator post with a single mauve band. Proceed over the brow of the hill with a view of the Hog's Back ahead, and continue down to a crosstrack. Turn left downhill still following mauve posts. After passing five mauve marker posts go past a gate [Hampton Estate - Puttenham Common marked on the other side]. Turn right onto a path, The North Downs Way.

2. After about 600 yards, travelling in an easterly direction, take a left fork signed North Downs Way, leaving the nature trail posts for the first time. After a short distance branch left at the Puttenham Common information board. Continue for almost $1/2$ mile and after passing some houses on the left immediately turn right over a stile, leaving the North Downs Way. Proceed across a field following a line of telegraph poles to the next stile at Lower Lascombe House.

3. Turn right, following a metalled lane for about 200 yards. Take a footpath to the left going diagonally right across a field to a stile under oak and pine trees. Cross diagonally left over a field to the next stile. Proceed along a path opposite with a beech hedge on the left to a Woodland Trust area. Carry straight on in a wooded area and go through a kissing gate where you turn left taking a wide path with a cottage and a house on the left. Follow this track for another two thirds of a mile, passing a chestnut paling fence on your left and Puttenham Common Top Car Park on your right. At this point new-comers to the area are advised to walk around the perimeter of the car park to take in the view.

Shorter version B - turn right beyond the Top Car Park and just before reaching the road. Then follow unmarked pathways keeping the road, Suffield Lane, close by on your left for about $1/2$ mile back to the Middle Car Park.

4. Cross over the road passing a single house on your left, veer left on a public footpath going down the slope where you turn left and immediately right. Follow a footpath up the hill and continue along with a chestnut paling fence on the right, through a wooden gate, [next to a cross country fence], and go over the stile ahead. Proceed down the left side of a field, over a stile and immediately turning 90 degrees right over another stile. Then negotiate three small stiles before reaching the road. Turn right along the road and take another right turn just past the pond. Walk along the metalled road with Lydling Farm on your right. Ignore a signposted public footpath to the left opposite a stone wall and keep straight on up the road which soon becomes an unmade track. Continue up the hill round a left and then a right bend and follow the path for some way to a crossways with an indicator post. Turn right on a bridleway for 350 yards before turning right again at the next signpost where you continue along a bridleway to a metalled road by Rodsall Manor.

5. Turn left for 75 yards and then turn left off the road following a bridleway until you pass over a stream with Willow Cottage and Garden Cottage on your left. At the end of the brick wall turn left on to a cinder track and follow this round the edge of Cutmill Pond. Cross a bridge over a stream and then a wide driveway, keeping ahead to a public bridleway through a silver birch wood. On reaching the road turn right. Continue along the grass verge at the side of the road to a crossroads and turn right. After passing Tarn Lake on the left turn left at a layby towards the lake, following a track with a wooden rail on the left. Turn right at the top of the steps continuing through to the starting point.

2 Compton – Loseley Park

Michael's walk

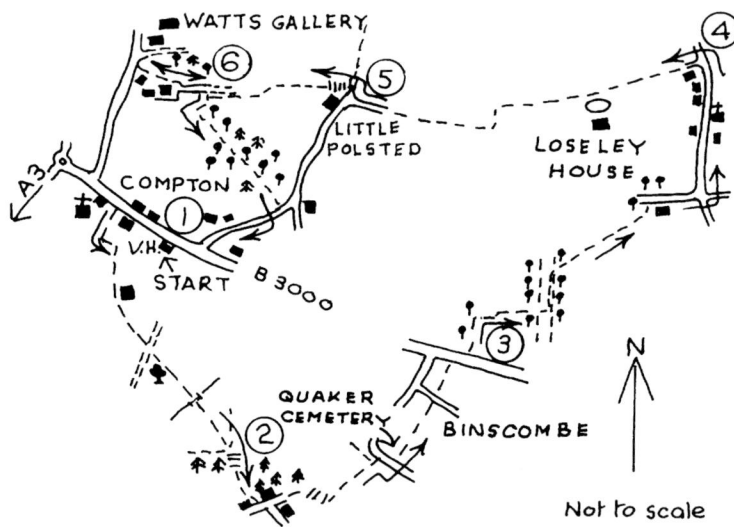

Length: 5 1/2 or 6 miles with visit to tea shop and Watts Gallery.
Maps: OS Landranger 186; Explorer 145.
Start: GR 958466 Compton Village Hall car park, on B3000. Take A3 south from Guildford or A3100 from Godalming.
Transport: Stagecoach and SCC buses Guildford - Godalming; or Tillingbourne buses Godalming - Farnham, to Compton.
Refreshments: The Tea Shop, Watts Gallery, open 10.30am to 5.30pm daily except 24th - 31st December inclusive. The Harrow Inn, Compton.
Introduction: This walk is a favourite of mine because it has a variety of terrain and countryside; it includes a tea shop; and I met Julia, now my wife!
Watts Gallery is a memorial to G.F. Watts, OM.RA. 1817-1904, a famous Victorian painter and sculptor. Open afternoons except Thursdays - tel. 01483 810235.

THE WALK

1. On the Compton Village Hall side of the road, with your back to it, turn left and walk towards the pub, The Harrow. Just beyond the car park entrance turn left down a track and follow it slightly right and then back left behind a holly bush, along the back of some gardens and over a concrete stile. Turn right and follow the righthand field edge. At the top of the field cross a track with a farm gate on the left and continue ahead down the side of the field to a stile. Cross the next field to a stile, slightly to the left of the trees ahead of you, onto a farm track. Cross this track into a field and aim slightly left of a tree on the brow of the hill. Continue beyond the brow and a metal kissing gate will come into view at the bottom of the field. Go through this gate into another field and uphill to the corner where a hedge and a wood meet. Climb over a stile and up steps.

2. Follow the path uphill through woods, passing gardens on the right, before coming to a metalled road. Turn left immediately down another path, next to a garden, and continue through woods and down some steps to a stile overlooking a field, Binscombe village, and a view to the Hog's Back. Go down the field and over a stile to a road. Turn right for 40 yards then left beside the Quaker cemetery, and follow a fence on the left side. Continue straight on until you reach a road running across in front of you. Cross this road and enter a recreation ground. Go straight across to a hedge/fence on the other side and out to a main road. Turn right along the verge 30 yards then cross the road, passing over a ditch and stile, into a field.

3. Follow the edge of the field straight ahead to the corner then turn right along the field boundary to a gap in the hedge. Go through this gap and turn right across the field until you reach a fingerpost by a cart track and gate. Turn left and follow the track for 100 yards then turn right and go over a stile in the hedge. Once in the field cross diagonally left between two large oaks to the far corner. In the corner follow the line of the fence for 25 yards then go right to a stile. Cross this into a field and again go diagonally left to a stile by a gate and down a short length of track to a metalled road. Turn right and proceed for $1/4$ mile to a T junction. Turn left and follow the road for about $1/2$ mile, past Littleton church on the right, to a junction next to a public telephone.

4. Turn left and follow a path over a stile and straight across a field to another stile. Over the next $1/2$ mile or so there are a number of fences to cross. Some are electrified, the crossing point marked by insulated rubber tubing, but be careful! Keep straight on crossing fields and stiles until you climb over a stile into a cart track. Follow the cart track to your right with a pond on your left. Continue in a straight line with a fence on the left until a fence blocks your route and there is a stile on your left. Climb the stile and turn right. Turn right again through a gate to another stile on the left and climb over. Follow the fence line round the lefthand corner until it reaches a stile. Go over stile and turn right until the path meets a track. Turn right along the track, under an avenue of trees, away from Loseley House. Follow the track for $1/2$ mile until it reaches houses at Little Polsted and a metalled road.

5. Turn right up a sunken path for 50 yards and then left up steps onto a fenced path. After about 400 yards go over a stile into a field. Follow a path for 300 yards then go over a stile onto a crossing path. [Note: you will be returning to this point if you visit Watts Gallery and/or the tea shop.]

6. To visit Watts Gallery and /or tea shop. Turn right and go over another stile onto a concrete road. Turn left towards farm buildings. Where the road turns left at farm buildings, leave it and turn right up a bank and over a stile on your left. Continue through holly woods to a road. Turn right along the road to reach Watts Gallery and the tea shop on the right.

To complete the walk retrace your steps, returning along the concrete road and turning right over the stile at the end, to the point noted earlier. Ignoring the stile on the left crossed earlier, follow a path round fields and through woods to a metalled road. Turn right along this to the main road, then right again to the Village Hall.

Shorter version omitting Watts Gallery and tea shop
Turn left on this crossing path and follow it round fields and through woods to a metalled road. Turn right along this to the main road, then right again to the Village Hall.

3 Godalming – North Downs Way – River Wey

Eric and Hazel's walk

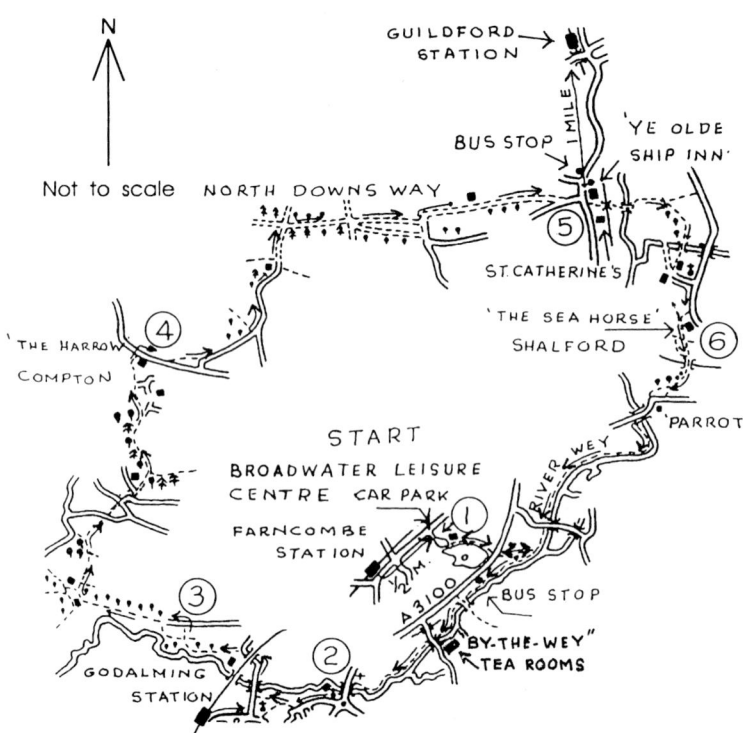

Length: 11 miles.

Maps: OS Landranger 186; Explorer 145.

Start: GR 982454 Broadwater Park Godalming Leisure Centre, Summers Road, Farncombe.

Transport: Buses between Godalming - Guildford. Join walk at points indicated on the map. Railway stations at Godalming, Farncombe or Guildford provide links as indicated on the map.

Refreshments: By-the-Wey Tea Rooms, Farncombe Boathouse. PHs The Harrow, Compton; Ye Olde Ship Inn, St. Catherine's, Guildford; The Sea Horse or The Parrot, Shalford.

Introduction: This is an easy walk with good views of the Hog's Back and North Downs. It provides a sense of history with the Pilgrims' Way included, and we like to think of the Pilgrims walking this route on their way to Canterbury. Ye Olde Ship Inn is a welcoming pub with good food served promptly and makes a good lunch stop.

THE WALK

1. Go out of the car park with the tennis courts on your right. Take the lefthand path and keep bearing left, past houses, and follow the path around Broad Water Lake until the main road [A3100] is reached. Cross the road to a fingerpost and stile opposite and follow a path to the River Wey. Go over a stile, turn right and follow the riverside footpath to Farncombe Boat House at Catteshall. Cross over the road and follow footpath past a lock on the lefthand side and beside water meadows, continuing past Sainsbury's on the opposite bank of the river, which bends right here to go into Godalming. Follow the footpath past the Godalming United Reformed Church on the right and out to a road [A3100].

2. Cross the main road and turn left over the bridge then bear right on a small path behind the library to a road. Turn right along the road passing the Borough Hall car park entrance, and reach a second car park, Crown Court, on the left. Keep ahead past this and soon take a footpath on the right towards the church. Fork right at a junction of paths and join Borough Road. Turn right and cross to a footpath on the lefthand side of the road which goes over the river, then through a private car park to rejoin the road just before a railway bridge. Go under the bridge and immediately turn left along a footpath. Cross a drive and continue along the path opposite. Follow the river staying on the tarmac path until it swings right to reach Peperharow Road.

3. Turn left to the end of the road and take the footpath ahead marked 'To Shackleford'. Continue along the path to reach a house, Milton Wood. Follow the boundary of the house, go through a handgate and bear right along a drive. Within 100 yards turn right on a path beside a walled garden and go gently uphill for 400 yards until you come to two paths 20 yards apart on the right, with marker posts. Ignoring the first post continue to the second and branch right on a bridleway and go up to a road. Cross to a bridleway opposite and continue up to a further road. Cross over and go along a drive opposite signed to The Spinney. Keep left past Broomfield Manor and at the end take a footpath ahead downhill. At the bottom of the hill go through a kissing gate on the left. Keeping the wood on your left, follow the field edge continuing on through a further kissing gate. Go up an incline and down the opposite side to a stile on the left beyond the wood and just past a field gate. Cross the stile and head diagonally down the field to another stile. Go up the lefthand edge of the next field and over the rise, passing farm buildings on your right. In the bottom corner turn left over a concrete stile and follow a path round beside gardens to reach The Harrow Inn in Compton village.

4. Cross the road. Turn right down to a telephone kiosk. Cross the green parallel to the road and join Polsted Lane. Go forward down the lane and bear left at a No Through Road sign. Walk up to Polsted Manor. Keep forward on a bridleway, passing a path off left, to a junction of paths. Turn right onto the North Downs Way [NDW]. At a fork keep on the broad track, bearing left and immediately right, still following NDW signs. At next junction turn left, still on the NDW, then soon right to pass Piccards Farm and join Sandy Lane. Turn left to reach the main road [A3100] and Ye Olde Ship Inn.

5. Cross the main road and turn right in front of the pub. After a few yards turn left into Ferry Lane with the ruins of St. Catherine's chapel on the right. Go down the lane over the railway bridge and down to the River Wey. Turn right and cross the bridge over the river and follow the path 50 yards to Shalford playing fields. Turn right beside the trees to the far righthand corner and take a footpath to the right leading through Shalford Water Works and passing Shalford church on the left. Reach a road [A281] and turn right.

6. Just before The Sea Horse pub take a bridleway on the right. Follow this round to Shalford Common having crossed a railway bridge. Cross the drive to Dagley Farm and follow the footpath opposite, past Juniper Cottages on the right, keeping forward until you join a road opposite The Parrot pub. Turn right along the road, cross the footbridge over the river and turn left across the road to a footpath opposite. Follow this alongside the River Wey on your left. Pass Unstead Lock and later cross a road to the footpath opposite, still following the river on your left until a stile on the right is reached. Go over the stile and follow a path to a stile beside the main road [A3100]. Cross the stile and go over the road to Broad Water Lake. Turn left and retrace your steps on the path going round the righthand side of the lake until the car park is reached.

4 Blackheath – Winterfold – Pitch Hill – Farley Green

George and Mary's walk

Length: 9 miles.
Maps: OS Landrangers 186 and 187; Explorer 145.
Start: GR 036462 Main car park at Blackheath east of The Villagers PH.
Transport: Train or bus to Chilworth railway station. Tillingbourne and London and Country bus service Guildford - Dorking/Cranleigh. Go over level crossing up Sampleoak Lane $3/4$ mile. Turn left at cross-roads and keep ahead to car park at Blackheath.
Refreshments: The Windmill PH near Ewhurst; The Villagers PH, Blackheath.

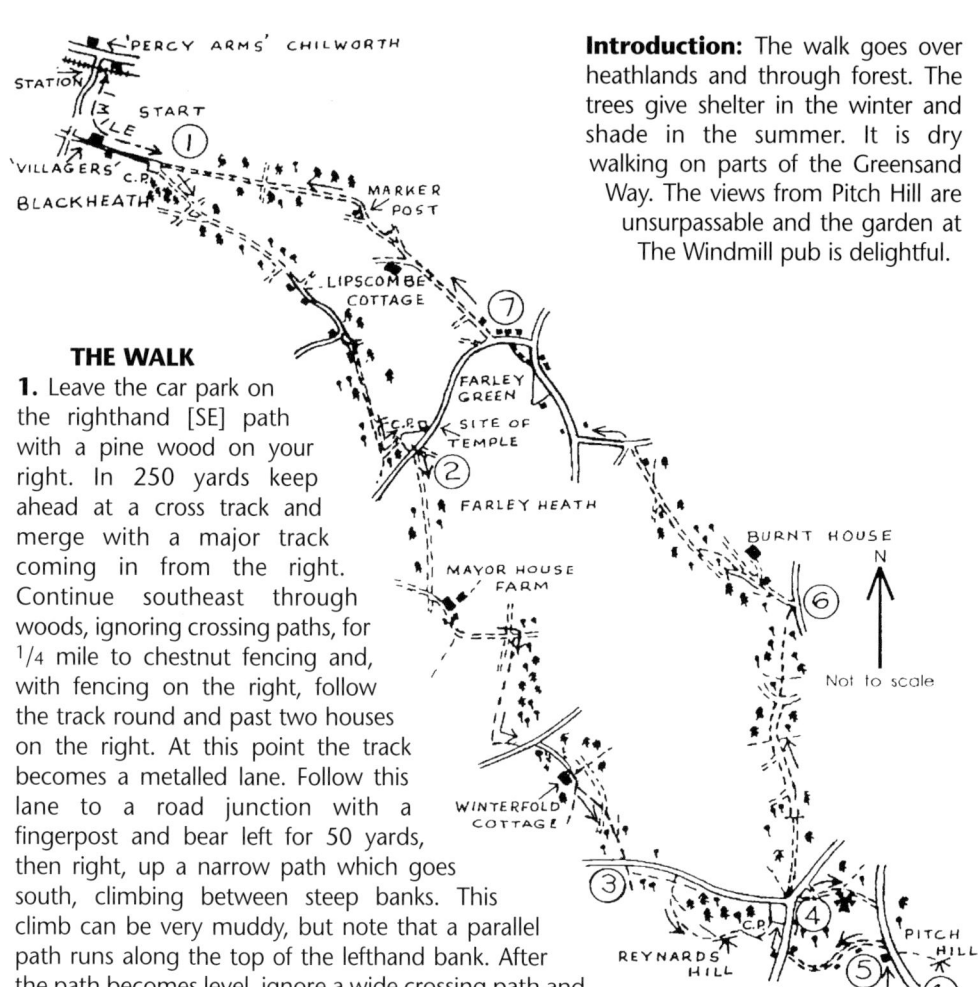

Introduction: The walk goes over heathlands and through forest. The trees give shelter in the winter and shade in the summer. It is dry walking on parts of the Greensand Way. The views from Pitch Hill are unsurpassable and the garden at The Windmill pub is delightful.

THE WALK

1. Leave the car park on the righthand [SE] path with a pine wood on your right. In 250 yards keep ahead at a cross track and merge with a major track coming in from the right. Continue southeast through woods, ignoring crossing paths, for 1/4 mile to chestnut fencing and, with fencing on the right, follow the track round and past two houses on the right. At this point the track becomes a metalled lane. Follow this lane to a road junction with a fingerpost and bear left for 50 yards, then right, up a narrow path which goes south, climbing between steep banks. This climb can be very muddy, but note that a parallel path runs along the top of the lefthand bank. After the path becomes level, ignore a wide crossing path and continue ahead on a broad sandy track for 200 yards to a junction with a gate on the right. Here the bridleway turns left and leads into a car park. [There is the site of a Roman Temple at the far end of the car park on the left.] On entering the car park bear right to a metal gate and cross the Farley Green - Shamley Green road at the fingerposts.

2. Continue south-east on the righthand track, through trees on Farley Heath, for 600 yards to a main east-west track and turn left. Pass Mayor House Farm and in 100 yards start descent and continue downhill to a sunken track, which is a bridleway. Cross this and turn right immediately on a footpath to walk south, parallel to the bridleway, for 1/2 mile to a stile. Turn left through woodland to a road. Cross the road into the drive to Winterfold Cottage. Keep left at the front gate to the house and follow a hedge for 70 yards, ignoring all paths to the left, until you reach an old garden gate on the right. Here bear left, [note: not sharp left] climbing through trees and crossing a wide access track, and continue ahead slightly right [SE] for 350 yards to a road which traverses the top of Winterfold Hill, opposite Jelley's Hollow.

3. Cross the road and turn left up a path signposted Greensand Way [GW], parallel with the road, for 300 yards to a crossing path. Turn right and ignoring the lefthand fork, follow a path which winds along the top of Reynards Hill [800 feet]. This woodland is part of the Hurtwood Control with views south over the weald to the South Downs. The path bears left to re-join the road by a small parking area, [car park 4].

4. Turn right, cross the Cranleigh - Shere road and go up a track for 300 yards to pass a windmill on the hilltop before dropping down by a fence on your right to the Ewhurst road. Turn right downhill for 300 yards to The Windmill PH for refreshments. There are excellent views from the pub garden to the south and south-west. The distance so far is $4^1/_2$ miles.

To enjoy the extensive views from the summit of Coneyhurst Hill at 843 feet, also known as Pitch Hill and marked 4A on map, take one of the paths just below the pub, on the opposite side of the road, that climb steeply to the top. Retrace your steps.

5. From the north side of the pub follow a narrow metalled road westwards [with pub on the left at first] for 600 yards to another road. Turn right uphill to the top and turn left at a road junction. Immediately take the righthand of two paths [a bridleway] and continue downhill ignoring side paths. After 500 yards the path goes through a gate and widens before being joined by a broad track from the left. Keep ahead downhill for 300 yards and pass another track coming in from the left. Continue ahead over a crossing footpath to a junction of forestry roads at the bottom and go ahead down between trees on a low lying path. Cross over a bridleway, go through a gate and keep ahead up a slope $^1/_4$ mile to reach a metalled drive, just short of a road on the right.

6. Turn left along the drive for 300 yards to the entrance of Burnt House, then 200 yards ahead bear left between holly bushes down a narrow path to a bridleway at the bottom. Turn right by a stream and after $^1/_4$ mile reach a track with a house on the left. Keep ahead, ignoring a right fork, to pass a house on the right and shortly meet a metalled lane. Here turn left for 200 yards to a T junction, then right into Farley Green village.

7. About 30 yards before the telephone kiosk, bear left along a sandy track on the left side of the green, then turn left along a road. At Westerlea Farm on the left, turn right onto the righthand of two tracks, marked as a bridleway. In 600 yards, on approaching Lipscombe Cottage and it's garages on the left, bear right up a sandy bridleway. Keep left at a fork passing a seat on the right. In 150 yards bear slightly left taking the centre one of three tracks ahead [W] and keeping a marker post on your right. Branch right at the next marker post, numbered 232, keeping this on your left. In 100 yards, at another marker post, go straight ahead still following path 232. After a further 450 yards join a broad track and at the next junction keep ahead on this but now following posts marked 302. Continue for $^1/_2$ mile to return to the car park at Blackheath.

Note. Walks 4 and 5 both explore Farley Heath and Winterfold Hill by different routes. They meet at the car park at Farley Heath [5:2 and 4:2] and at Jelley's Hollow [5:4 and 4:3]. See sketch maps.

5 Blackheath – Winterfold – Smithwood Common – Shamley Green

William's walk

Length: 12½ miles.

Maps: OS Landrangers 186 and 187; Explorer 145.

Start: GR 037462 Main car park at Blackheath east of The Villagers PH.

Transport: Train or bus to Chilworth railway station. Tillingbourne or London and Country buses Guildford - Dorking and Cranleigh, or SCC Leisure buses summer Sundays. Go over level crossing and up Sampleoak Lane for ¾ mile. Turn left at crossroads up to car park at Blackheath. To join at Smithwood Common [5] use Tillingbourne buses from Guildford via Cranleigh - Ewhurst - Bramley.

Refreshments: Bricklayers Arms PH, Shamley Green; The Villagers PH, Blackheath at end of walk. The top of Jelley's Hollow, overlooking a splendid view of the South Downs, makes a good picnic spot [see 4 on map].

Introduction: This is one of my favourite walks and can be enjoyed all year round. It is perhaps best at bluebell time, but it is beautiful with the heather in August and in snow. There are lots of ups and downs and one long flat stretch. You get views of the North Downs from Blackheath and Farley Heath and of the South Downs when you join the Greensand Way at Winterfold. Jelley's Hollow can be muddy but the bluebells are at their best here and worth the effort. Spring flowers accompany us to Smithwood Common and we then walk the disused railway [Horsham to Guildford line] and see the river and the old Wey and Arun canal which is slowly being restored. There are hills on either side; don't forget to look back on Plonks Hill and name them all.

THE WALK

1. From the car park take the large sandy track east by a bridleway 302 post, next to a gate. Keep to this bridleway for about a mile, going straight on and ignoring paths off to the right and left. When the path starts to narrow and forks, go right with the main track. At a clearing at the next fork keep left, with silver birches between the fork, and head towards a sandy track opposite [SE]. Cross the junction of five paths on the sandy track. After 35 yards turn right down a narrow grass track in the bracken. Go downhill [S] to join the drive to a house, Remnants, in the bottom. Turn right on a grassy track and follow it for 175 yards to a crossing track with a waymark to your right. Turn left on a bridleway, shortly going uphill through woodland. Keep straight on to cross a wide sandy track [beware of traffic] and at a quick fork keep right, uphill, on a bridlepath. Keep straight on, passing a house in the woods to your left, and follow the path until the car park on Farley Heath is reached. [Over to the left are the remains of a Romano-British temple [circa 100AD]. The walls are just above ground level.] Keep ahead along the righthand edge of the car park to a gate by a road.

2. Cross the road to a gate opposite. Take the bridleway to the right, uphill, ignoring a path off to the left. At a sandy crossing track [bridleway 229] keep ahead and go up the path opposite. Go straight over at the next junction of paths and crossing track and in 30 yards fork left, leaving the signed bridleway on your right. Continue uphill, looking back for views to the North Downs. Near the top of the rise at a four path junction, take the path on the left with fields and a fence on your left. The view to the left includes Ranmore Church, Mayor House Farm and the North Downs. A mass of bluebells starts here and later the blackberries are delicious! When the track turns right, cross a stile by a gate and go down the righthand side of a field, passing a stile on the right. Go downhill to the next field and cross a stile by a gate. Keeping to the right of the field pass a gate and sheds to cross another stile in the corner of the field. Follow a narrow path into the woods. Keep straight on when a bridleway joins from the right. At a six path junction go straight on uphill on a stony track fourth from the left. Later on ignore a path on the right and pass stables on your left. At a junction with a rough lane cross to the footpath opposite and go through the woods. The path swings left to reach a road at a footpath sign.

3. Cross the road to a narrow grassy track which swings right just before a lone pine tree. Follow the track to another road and cross into a lay-by and parking area. Take a narrow footpath at the righthand end. Keep forward, ignoring lefthand turns, then bear right at a crossing path to go down over several bumps and reach a large car park on Winterfold Hill. Turn left to the end of the car park and a Hurtwood Control sign. Walk forward to a grand viewpoint - with a seat provided! Return to the Hurtwood Control sign and take a path going left from the end of the car park and behind the seat. In about 20 yards there is a marker post with a GW sign on the yellow arrow. [This is the Greensand Way (GW) which you now follow to a road at the top of Jelley's Hollow - 4 on map.] When the path forks [no marker] go right. Keep forward, following GW signs at intervals and ignoring paths off to either side, on a narrow, undulating and winding path which keeps along the side of the hill, with the slope down to your right. When you join a larger path, by a GW marker post, bear right uphill but mind the pits dug beside the path. Cross another car park, enjoying the views to the right, and keep ahead along the main path, ignoring a path downhill to the right. Continue following the broad path and ignore side paths. Swing left with the path at a GW post to go up a slope, ignoring a path to the right. After 50 yards cross a narrow lane and continue on a small path opposite, by a GW marker. Follow this path that wanders down, via wooden steps, to reach a road by a GW marker post at the top of Jelley's Hollow.

4. Turn sharp right downhill through Jelley's Hollow, there is no need to touch the road, and keep to the main track for 1^1/$_4$ miles. The bluebells are at their best here. Dogs and geese guard the house partway down the hollow but are securely locked in. The main track has high wire fences on either side, not very attractive. Ignore the drive [a bridleway] on the left after the big house. At the end of a straight path bend right and then left, crossing a track just before going through wooden bars onto a narrow path. There are open fields on both sides of the path now. At a second set of wooden bars turn sharp right [W]. Do not go towards the farm. Pass a gate on the right and follow a path which runs between a hedge and fence to a stile. Cross this and immediately cross a second stile then go straight over a field to cross another stile, keeping the fence on your left. The path goes alongside woods. Keep straight on and out into fields, passing under electrical lines. There are fine views here! At a crossing of tracks go straight on keeping the lines to your left and ignoring a track, right, to the farm. At a road turn right and after the gates to Alderbrook cross the road to a path in front of houses.

5. Follow the path along the edge of the green, crossing drives and passing houses on your left. Go straight on between posts to a field, continuing forward with a garden and a large house on your left. Follow the path between more posts and rails to reach the busy Cranleigh - Bramley road. Go down Rowly Drive opposite. This is just over ^{1}/$_2$ mile long and then becomes the driveway of Rowly Farm. Turn left at a water trough just before the farm. After about 40 yards take a bridleway to your right with fields left and farm buildings right. Pass between a hedged garden on the left and a house on your right to reach open fields. Go forward into the field and partway across, in a hollow, note a horse jump designed as a miniature timbered house! Turn left by a waymark and walk down to trees. Go over a stile before turning right.

6. You are now on the route of the old Horsham - Guildford railway and will follow it for the next 1^1/$_4$ miles - the flat part of the walk you were promised! The first bridge takes you over the river which meanders to your right. At the second bridge the bed of the old canal is on your left and the next bridge is where the canal went under the railway. Keep straight on under the first bridge over the railway track, which takes the Run Common road. Pass Rushett Farm on your left and cross a bridge over a farm track. The old canal bed can now be seen on the right. Go under the next bridge and almost immediately turn right up the slope to join the lane over the bridge. Turn left with the bed of the old canal on your right. Do not enter the caravan site but turn right, keeping up the fieldside with a hedge on your left. At the corner of the hedge keep forward across the field and go down over a ditch to reach the river. Keep forward, with the river to your right and past an old timber bridge into a field, to cross a second bridge over the river and into woodland. Continue on an uphill path through woods to Long Common ignoring several paths coming in from the right. Join a broad track and keep forward. Soon, with Long Common Cottage on your immediate left, branch right over the grass to a metal gate. Turn right to go through this and up to Plonks Hill between fences. The views back are marvellous, a run of hills from Hascombe Hill curving round to St. Martha's. At a crossing sandy track go straight on through a gate [NE] to reach a road. Cross over to Shamley Green church.

17

7. Take the footpath opposite between fences, passing through three kissing gates dedicated to E.W. (Tony) Parker OBE 1908 - 1994, a prominent member of the Kingston group of the Ramblers' Association. Reach a T junction and turn right. This path becomes a driveway through chestnut trees. Keep left at a junction of drives. Reel Hall on the left is an interesting building. Turn left onto a road and quickly right up a steep narrow bridleway. The path goes straight up to begin with then swings to the left. At a junction of paths keep to the main one going uphill to the right. With fields on both sides now, follow a sunken path and enjoy the views back to the South Downs. At the top of the hill turn left on a crossing track passing a house and farm on the left. The North Downs and Newlands Corner can be seen to the right. Just over the top of the rise take a footpath which curves right and passes between two metal gates. Follow it down to a road, first between wire fences then wooden ones. Rabbits galore here! Meet the road at Blackmoor Lodge.

8. Turn right and pass the drive to Sandhurst on the right and to Haldish Farm on the left. At the brow of the hill, between two metal gates, turn left down a driveway, signed as a footpath, to Darbyn's Brook. Go downhill passing a house on the right. Keeping forward on their driveway go round by a lake watching for black swans and other birds. Swing left to reach a road. Turn right uphill and pass Hallams Farm house. About 200 yards further on, where electricity lines cross the road, turn sharp right up a narrow, steep, sunken path. There is a small pylon on the hill ahead. This is bridleway P1 and there is a marker post about 20 yards in from the road. Follow this bridleway uphill and leftish through woodland. Cross a stony driveway and continue on bridleway P1 opposite. Keep forward over the top of the rise ignoring paths either side. At a five path junction take the first path left which soon takes you to the cricket pitch on Blackheath. Keep to the right of the pitch to join a small road. Go straight on to a larger road and the car park you started from is on your right. The cricket ground is well used so you might be able to watch a couple of overs whilst you relax your toes. Hope you enjoyed the walk!

6 Newlands Corner – St Martha's Church – Tilling Bourne Valley – Chilworth

Roger and Margaret's walk

Length: 6³/₄ or 7¹/₂ miles including Chilworth.
Maps: OS Landranger 186, Explorer 145.
Start: GR 044492 Newlands Corner car park on A25 Guildford to Dorking road. To join the walk from Chilworth railway station [GR 031473] turn left and take a path on the right just beyond the school, signed Vera's Path. This leads to a footbridge and the main route at 4A on the map.
Transport: London and Country Surrey Hills Leisure Bus to Newlands Corner on Sundays and public holidays in summer. Also regular Tillingbourne/London and Country buses and rail service to Chilworth.
Refreshments: Two cafés at Newlands Corner at start/finish of the walk. Also diversion to Percy Arms PH, Chilworth possible [see 4A map and text].

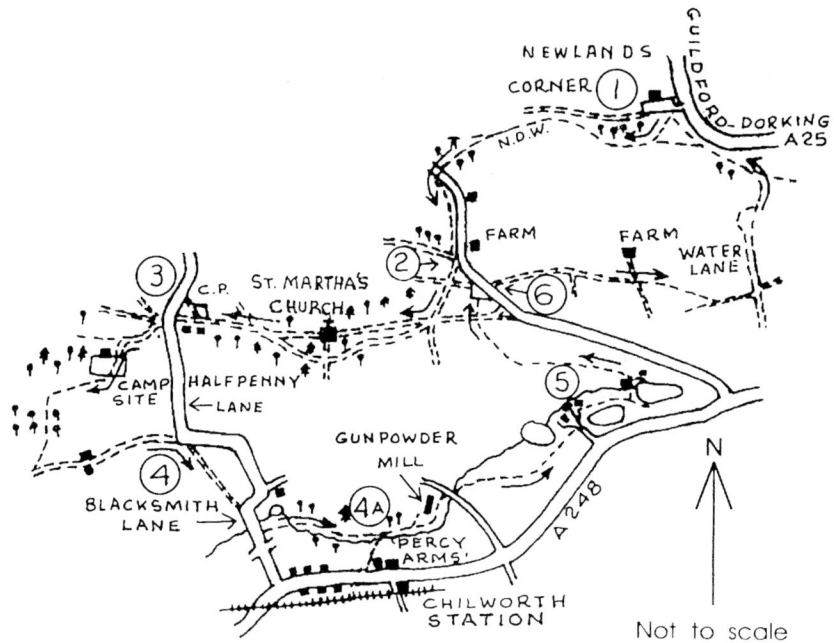

Not to scale

Introduction: The walk provides a variety of terrain; grassland, woodland and lakes. Herons can often be seen by the first of the Postford ponds. There are fine views from Newlands Corner, St Martha's church and the Downs beyond Halfpenny Lane. The industrial archaeology of the Tilling Bourne valley with the remains of powder mills for example, is of interest. The ground over most of the route is well drained and therefore rarely muddy. The walk has several steep parts in the last two miles which some might find strenuous.

THE WALK

1. From Newlands Corner to Halfpenny Lane the route follows that of the North Downs Way [NDW], a long distance footpath waymarked with the conventional acorn sign. From near the road end of the car park go down over a picnic area to a footpath which bears right through trees. Follow this past waymarks to open downland and take one of several grassy tracks running below the wood. After about 1/2 mile from Newlands Corner take a footpath going obliquely to a wood on the left [acorn sign] and go through this to a road. Cross the road and turn left onto a footpath running alongside it. Pass a farm on the left and shortly afterwards reach a junction of tracks with the road.

2. Take the track leading up the hill [NDW sign] and ignoring side paths reach a broad cross track in 325 yards. Turn right onto this and follow it uphill to St Martha's church. Here a memorial to Yvonne Arnaud may be seen in the churchyard. Beyond the church continue in the same general direction along a broad track down through a wood at first and then along the left side of an open area to reach a drive with a car park on the right. Go over the drive and down to a road, Halfpenny Lane.

3. Turn left along the road and almost immediately right through a gateway. Ignoring a track going right, follow one leading south-west past No Horses, No Bicycles signs. After about 160 yards take a left fork and arrive at the corner of a campsite. A hut will be seen on the right. Cross the field to a stile and bear right to follow a grassy track to a belt of trees and on to a second belt or line of trees. Turn left here and go directly downhill through a wood to a stile at the edge of a field. Cross the stile and go diagonally right to a junction with a main track. Turn left along the track and continue to meet Halfpenny Lane again.

4. Go right along the road and almost immediately right again onto a footpath leading to the junction of Halfpenny Lane and Blacksmith Lane. Go along Blacksmith Lane and almost immediately cross the Tilling Bourne. Eighty yards beyond the river turn left through a metal gateway and follow the footpath through the wood to reach a footpath on the right leading to a footbridge.

4A. Diversion/return to Chilworth - take this footpath on the right and go over the footbridge. Take the path straight ahead between fields. Pass a school and at the A248 turn left for The Percy Arms PH and the rail station. Retrace your steps to rejoin the route.

To continue the main route keep ahead and go to the right of the derelict gunpowder mill buildings. On reaching a lane turn right and shortly left to a stile. Continue over fields and two more stiles and pass a large pond on the left. A fourth stile gives access to a footpath running between trees and a wire fence. A lane with a pond opposite, Postford Pond, is soon reached. Go left along the lane between the pond and houses and in about 200 yards reach another pond, Watreloo Pond. Keep left of the pond and just beyond a house go left along a footpath leading west through a wood.

5. Continue through the wood to a field boundary where the footpath bears right and goes more steeply uphill away from the field. Near the top of the slope ignore minor footpaths leading off right and left. On reaching a T junction with a main track, go straight ahead over grass for 80 yards to the edge of a car park. From here a footpath goes right. Follow this to a road.

6. Cross the road and continue along the bridleway opposite. At a cross track leading to a farm go ahead through a gate and cross a field to a gate in the field boundary. Turn left here onto a footpath and go through another gate and thence down to a lane, Water Lane. Turn left along the lane and go straight on ignoring a track immediately on the right. Where the lane bears left, keep straight on up the hill. In 200 yards bear right, then left at a clearing and chalk pit. Continue uphill along the track which gradually approaches the A25 and reach the starting point.

7 Abinger Roughs – Abinger Common – Wotton

Audrey's walk

Length: 5^3/$_4$ miles or 6 miles with a visit to the Stephan Langton Inn and the Mill Pond, Friday Street.

Maps: OS Landranger 187; Explorer 146.

Start: GR 111480 Abinger Roughs NT car park, White Down Lane, off A25 ^{3}/$_4$ mile east of Abinger Hammer and signposted Effingham. The car park is ^{1}/$_2$ mile up the road on the left.

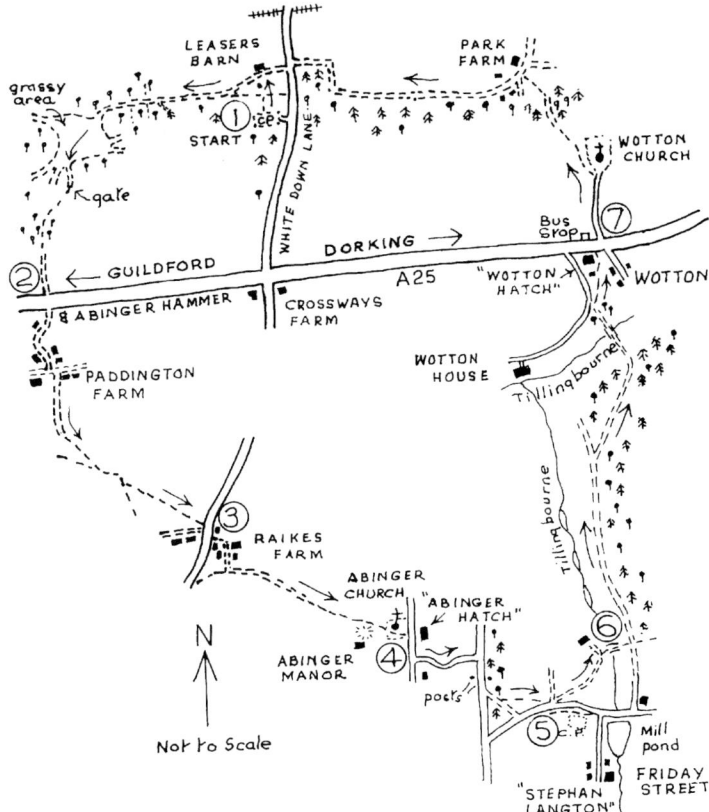

Transport: Tillingbourne London & Country buses between Guildford and Dorking along A25. Alight at Wotton Hatch Hotel and start the walk at 7.

Refreshments: Abinger Hatch PH, The Stephan Langton Inn [detour], Wotton Hatch Hotel.

Introduction: A favourite walk for all seasons with beautiful views up to the North Downs. It's easy walking and usually dry even in winter due to the mainly sandy soil. There are bluebells in the spring, coolness and shade by the pretty Tillingbourne stream in the summer and in the autumn wonderful colours in the beech woods.

THE WALK

1. Take the path between wooden fence posts off the north side of the car park nearly at the end on the right hand side. Go straight over the rise and descend to Leasers Barn and the Wilberforce Memorial which marks the spot where Bishop Wilberforce was thrown from his horse and killed in 1837. At the memorial turn left along the track, keeping parallel with the field edge. Ignoring a large path coming in left and other side turnings, keep forward on the main track going uphill and continuing to a large, flat grassy area. Cross this and at the far side turn left on a track with a marker post and white arrow. Go through the gate ahead and keep to a path around the top of an open field. Follow the path through a gate and down a sunken path between hedges to the A25.

2. Cross with great care and take the metalled bridleway opposite leading round to Paddington Farm. Turn left beyond the farm buildings, by the large farmhouse, then shortly

21

right on a bridleway. Keep ahead for about ½ mile. Just beyond the top of the hill the path swings left and then right. Here, look for a broken gate and a gap in the hedge on the left, by a holly tree. Turn left through the gap and follow a path bearing slightly right across two fields towards farm buildings, to emerge in Raikes Lane.

3. Turn right along the lane and almost immediately turn left onto a path beside Stable Cottage. In the farm yard turn right, following yellow arrows, down a track to the left of Raikes Farmhouse. Follow this track as it swings sharply left where a footpath joins uphill from the right. The track is at first between hedges and then fences with open fields either side and extensive views all around and especially to the North Downs away on the left. Continue forward across an open field with the houses of Abinger Common visible ahead. Cross a stile and keep alongside a hedged garden on the right, with a motte making an interesting and unusual feature, to reach Abinger Church, dedicated to St. James, the patron of pilgrims. and which suffered bomb damage in the war. Go through the churchyard and out into a lane by a duck pond opposite Abinger Hatch PH.

4. Turn right along the lane and soon turn left into a smaller lane alongside the end of the pub garden and beside a house, Mark Ash. Follow this to a T junction with Hollow Lane. Turn right and just past some wooden posts either side of the road, marked Manor Gate, take a bridleway on the left. Go left at a Y fork and follow a path which descends and then bears left and is soon parallel with a small road on the right. Join the road at Mundies Farm track.

5. To visit Friday Street and the Stephan Langton Inn. Turn left along the road using a path on top of the bank on the right. Continue past the Friday Street NT car park on the right and descend to meet the lane where a bridleway joins from the right. Keep on downhill to the Mill Pond. The Stephan Langton Inn is a short way up the track to the right of the pond.

Continue the walk from the lane across the northern end of the pond by taking the broad track, alongside a red letter box inserted into a stone gate post, at Pond Cottage. Keep forward along this valley track and pass a stone bridge over the Tillingbourne on your left. Cross a stile by the gate ahead and continue from 6.

To complete the route omitting Friday Street and The Stephan Langton Inn. Immediately turn left by a fingerpost, down a drive signed 'Pugs Corner'. The drive ends at a house where our path turns right just before the gate. Cross a stone bridge over the Tillingbourne stream. Ignore the uphill path straight ahead and turn left over a stile by a gate. Continue at 6.

6. Follow a broad leafy path along the valley. In about 500 yards turn right uphill through Damphurst Wood on a broad fenced path. Continue ahead and descend into the valley of another branch of the Tillingbourne stream. Cross a stile and follow a fenced path across a bridge over the stream with another stile ahead. Go uphill through a small wood and over another stile alongside the drive to Wotton House. The path goes across a pasture and through a gate into the car park of the Wotton Hatch Hotel. Walk out to the road (A25) and cross over.

7. Bus travellers join the walk here. Take the drive opposite the pub, to reach Wotton church. Follow a footpath, as waymarked, over a stile on the lefthand side of the church wall. The church is usually closed but the porch of the south doorway is worth a visit. The arch over the inner door bears fascinating carvings including eight tiny three-inch heads, six of them 13th century, depicting king, peasant, archbishop etc. The origins are a mystery but may well have connections with (Bishop) Stephen Langton. Return to the footpath by the church wall and follow it across an open field with more extensive views to the Downs. The path goes over a stile and, now fenced, along the edge of woodland with bluebells flowering in the spring. Through the wood cross yet another stile into a field and follow a path diagonally left which leads to Park Farm. After another stile in the corner of the field take the second track on the left going between barns with Park Farm House and Cottage on the right. This track goes along the boundary edge of Deerleap Wood. Follow it until the lane to Effingham is reached. Turn left and immediately right on a path through the common leading back to the Wilberforce Memorial. Turn left up the hill and retrace your steps to the car park.

8 Ranmore – North Downs Way – Polesden Lacey

John and Joyce's walk

Length: 6¾ miles.

Maps: OS Landranger 187; Explorer 146.

Start: GR 142503 Denbies Hillside NT car park at east end of Ranmore Common Road [£1 charge for non-members].

Transport: SCC Surrey Hills Leisure buses from railway stations at Guildford, Dorking and Redhill serve this area on summer Sundays. Train to station at Boxhill and Westhumble then walk 1¾ miles to join route at 3A [see map].

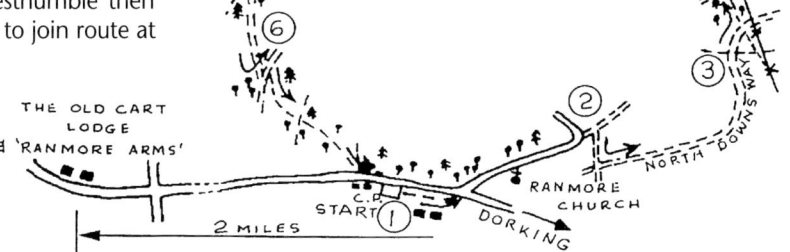

Refreshments: Polesden Lacey NT restaurant - see members' handbook or telephone 01372 456190 for opening times [£3.00 charge for non-members to enter grounds]. Also, 2 miles from start [see map] are The Ranmore Arms PH, Ranmore Common Road, and The Old Cartlodge Tea Rooms, Dunley Hill Farm, Crooknorth Road, open March - mid Dec Tues to Sun 10am - 4.30pm; Feb Wed to Sun 10am - 4.30pm for coffee, lunches, teas. [Closed mid-Dec to Feb. Tel 01483 282222]

23

Introduction: This walk is best in spring, summer and autumn. The terrain is varied and there are extensive views. The route passes near Polesden Lacey House [NT property] and the largest vineyard in the South of England, Denbies.

THE WALK

1. Leave car park, turning right towards Dorking, along a gravelled drive in front of houses on your right, until the track meets the Ranmore Common Road. Cross to a minor road opposite, passing Ranmore Church, St. Barnabas', on the right, and in about 600 yards, where the road bears left, continue ahead through a white barrier following North Downs Way [NDW] signpost.

2. In 30 yards turn right to follow NDW along a lane between fields. Soon after the lane descends turn left through a metal gate to follow the NDW along a wide track, passing through large gates securing the Denbies Wine Estate. There are good views of Dorking to the right and of vineyards covering the valley. The path descends gradually and turns north offering good views of Boxhill ahead, the A24, the railway and Denbies HQ.

3. Continue ahead over a crosspath with a clear view of Denbies HQ on the right, to reach a second crosspath with power lines almost overhead. Bear left, leaving the NDW, to follow a footpath with power lines now on your right. Go uphill through gateposts [no gates] and straight on to join a wide roadway from the left until you pass a large, dead tree trunk standing on the left. About 20 yards beyond this bear left along an easily missed path, following a wooden rail fence to reach a stile. Cross this and then follow the power lines with wooden poles across pasture to a stile at the corner of two fields. Cross the stile and follow a narrow path alongside a barbed wire fence. At the end pass through a squeeze and follow the field fence on the right to reach a stile and cross into a minor road. Turn right along this road to reach a T junction [3A]. Turn left and in 20 yards cross a stile into a field on the right. Walk uphill to a stile following the direction of the fingerpost to the right of the stile and gate. Cross the stile and continue uphill in the same direction on a narrow path through woods, to join a wider, grassy path. Turn left and just past a seat on the lefthand side reach a crosspath and turn left to reach a road.

4. Cross to a bridleway opposite, entering a drive to Bagden Farm. At the corner of a barn turn right, pass through two gates to emerge onto a track between fields, then go ahead to reach a gate at the end of the field. Pass through and turn right uphill passing under a road bridge. Continue on track NNW for about 3/4 mile to reach Polesden Road. Cross to the opposite side, turn left and follow a bridlepath parallel to the road which carries visitors to Polesden Lacey.

5. Where the road bears left keep ahead to follow a track towards Home Farm and Yew Tree Farm. After passing a triangle of grass on your left reach a junction of tracks and continue to follow track to Home Farm and Yew Tree Farm. After passing under a thatched bridge, in 200 yards bear right to follow a path through yew trees. After a metalled road joins from the left pass Yew Tree Farm on

24

lefthand side and in a short distance reach a fork. Take the main path left and uphill. In about 200 yards look back left between trees to see good views of Polesden Lacey House.

6. After passing through a metal gate across the track continue about 80 yards to reach a second wooden barrier on the lefthand side. Go left on a sandy path which first turns sharply back left and then right to head SE. Drop down to a valley, go over a crosspath at the bottom and then climb steeply uphill to follow a path through woodland to reach Ranmore Common Road. Pass through a barrier, bear left and follow a NT bridlepath parallel to the road, then cross to the car park opposite.

9 Blackbrook – Coldharbour – Leith Hill – Holmwood Common

Olga's walk

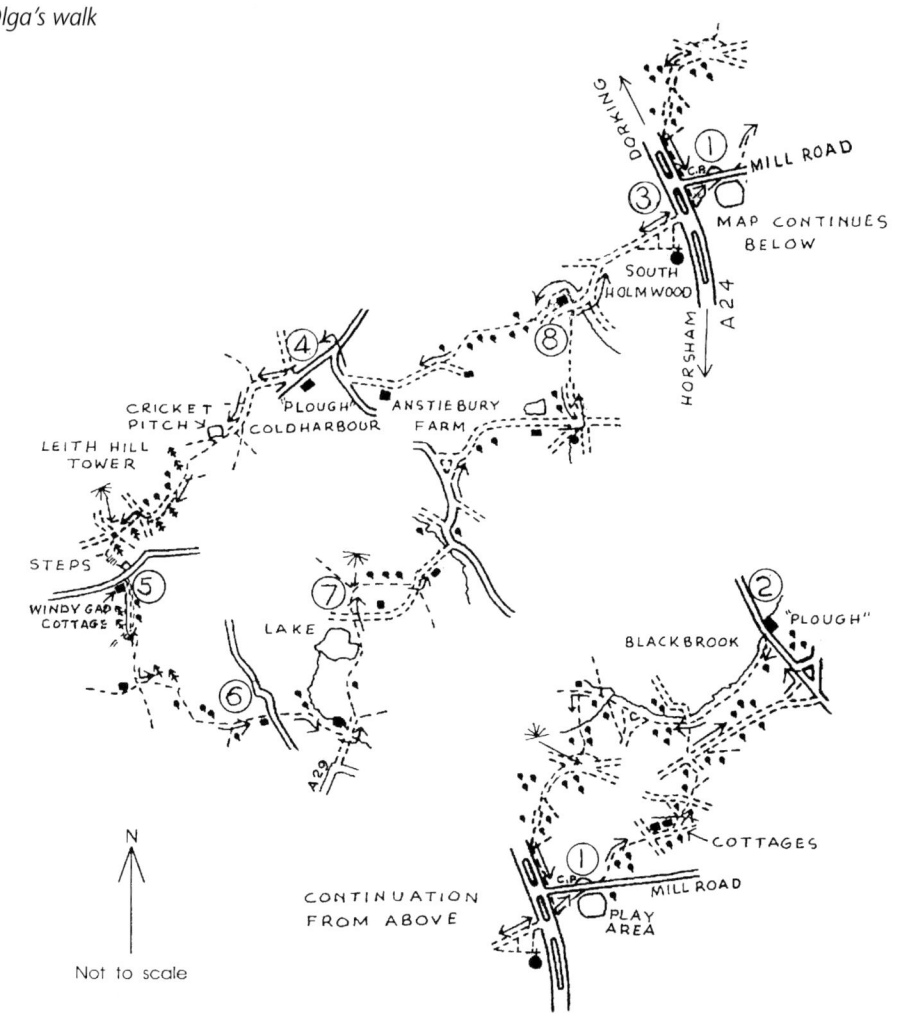

Length: 10 miles or two shorter versions: version A 2$^1/_2$ miles, sections 1 and 2 or version B 7$^1/_2$ miles, sections 3 to 8.

Maps: OS Landranger 187; Explorer 146.

Start: GR 172451 Mill Road car park, South Holmwood, just off southbound A24.

Transport: London & Country buses to South Holmwood [A24] by War Memorial and pedestrian underpass [3]. SCC Surrey Hills Leisure Buses to Leith Hill on Summer Sundays.

Refreshments: The Plough PH, Blackbrook; Plough Inn, Coldharbour; Leith Hill Tower NT kiosk - restricted opening in winter.

Introduction: The walk is varied, including field paths, woodland and farm tracks. Holmwood Common is criss-crossed with quiet paths with sunny, open spaces. It can however be rather wet in winter. The route undulates, following the high ground, including Leith Hill, the highest point in Surrey, 1029 feet from the top of the tower. In a few places there are some steep climbs. Throughout the walk there are extensive views across Surrey and Sussex, first to the South Downs and later to the North Downs. The views across to the wooded slopes of Leith Hill are superb in autumn. The Plough at Blackbrook is a cosy, sunny pub which serves excellent food, while The Plough at Coldharbour is a popular pub and conveniently placed. The kiosk in Leith Hill Tower provides a welcome rest and refreshments.

THE WALK

1. From the car park walk down the grass beside the road, away from the A24, for about 50 yards to a fingerpost on the same side. Turn left and follow the track, soon bearing right downhill to reach The Mill Cottage. Bear round right and continue past Clematis Cottage and Old Cottage, until the path soon divides. Take the lefthand track over the footbridge and bear right uphill past a waymark post. Continue forward to reach a broad double crosstrack. Bear right and immediately left onto a narrow track, continuing in the same general direction as before. Follow this track, which can be very wet in winter, ignoring a right fork and all side paths, to reach a main ride. Turn right and follow this broad ride to the Blackbrook Road. Go left along the road to the Plough Inn. [Caution is needed as the traffic tends to be fast along this road.]

2. Take a footpath directly opposite the pub which runs alongside the Black Brook. Continue along this path for a little over $^1/_2$ mile to a footbridge with handrails. In about 150 yards turn left onto a well defined track and continue until it becomes a grassy slope. Go forward up the slope to reach an open area where there is a tree with a bench seat below. There are fine views of the North Downs here. Pass to the left of this tree and keep forward to take a level grassy track indicated by a blue NT waymark. Ignore any side tracks until a fork is reached. Here bear right and right again to reach the A24. Walk in the direction of the traffic on a grassy path beside the road as far as Mill Road.

[**Shorter version A** - turn up Mill Road a short way to the car park. **Shorter version B** - start the walk from the car park by crossing the road and taking a small path opposite going diagonally right. Follow this round to the War Memorial and the A24 underpass.]

3. Continue a few yards to the underpass, cross the A24 and walk along Betchets Green Road through South Holmwood, with the church over to your left. Pass Betchets Green Farm and soon after this follow the road round to the left. Continue on the road past a house, Betchets Green, on the right and reach a gateway by East Lodge and a sign 'Private Road to Anstie Grange'. Turn right here over a stile and bear round to the left alongside the garden and up the lefthand edge of the field, continuing up through woodland. Continue climbing past a house and on up to reach and pass through Anstiebury Farm. Walk along the concrete drive to reach the road. Go right and shortly left onto the road which takes you into Coldharbour.

4. At the Plough Inn take the rough track opposite and with the telephone box on your left, walk steeply uphill. Where the path forks keep right and still uphill, following a sign 'To Tower and Cricket Ground'. By the cricket ground take a waymarked path left and soon right and follow this waymarked trail around the contours of Leith Hill. When this path comes out into the open there are splendid views to the South Downs and Leith Hill Tower can be glimpsed over the trees. Now the path drops down to a junction of six paths. Take the third path left very steeply uphill to reach the tower. Here a pause for refreshment will be welcome and the ascent of the tower [NT] affords a splendid all round view. Just beyond the tower turn left and following signs to Windy Gap car park, descend a flight of steps and reach a road.

5. Cross the road to a fingerpost by Windy Gap Cottage. Follow a track downhill to 'woodland walk' post 2. Turn left down a path between the trees which leads over a plank bridge to a stile. Cross into a field and continue downhill bearing left to a gate and stile immediately below a line of fir trees. Go over the stile and keep forward to reach a copse on your righthand side after about 200 yards. Turn right onto a track through this copse and continue until a cross track is reached. Here turn left as waymarked and continue into a field. After a short distance cross a stile on the left and go through a small copse and up a field to a stile which leads into the garden of a house. Cross into the garden and go straight forward to the drive which brings you to a road.

6. Turn right and immediately left to follow a field boundary on your left which curves round till houses are reached. At a drive to the main road [A29] turn left through Buckinghill Farm. Go through the gate and continue forward across the field to a second field. Keep to the righthand side of this field, beside the trees and look for a gate into a third field. This gate is beside Broome Hall Lake [not always visible in summer]. Continue half left to a stile into a narrow lane. Cross the stiles on either side and go directly forward uphill to reach the trees at the top. Pause here for excellent views to the south and west.

7. Go right keeping the field boundary on the left and cross three stiles to reach a lane. Go left through Bearehurst and follow the drive to the road. Turn left up the road for about 1/2 mile. Take the second fingerpost right, by Stable Cottage, and continue along this bridleway, passing a lake down on the left and Moorhurst Manor on the right, until a junction of footpaths is reached. Turn left along a lane in front of houses. Keep forward bearing slightly right uphill to a gate into a field. With the hedge on your left cross three fields to reach a stile and cross into a lane by East Lodge.

8. Turn right and retrace your steps along the lane into South Holmwood. [To see the church turn right at the third fingerpost, just after crossing a small stream. This path leads directly to the church. Leave the churchyard on the path to the left beside the church.] Make for the underpass to cross the A24. Once across, go up the steps by the War Memorial and circle left around a grassy play area to reach Mill Road opposite the car park.

27

10 Friday Street – Leith Hill – Holmbury – Abinger Common

John and Joyce's walk

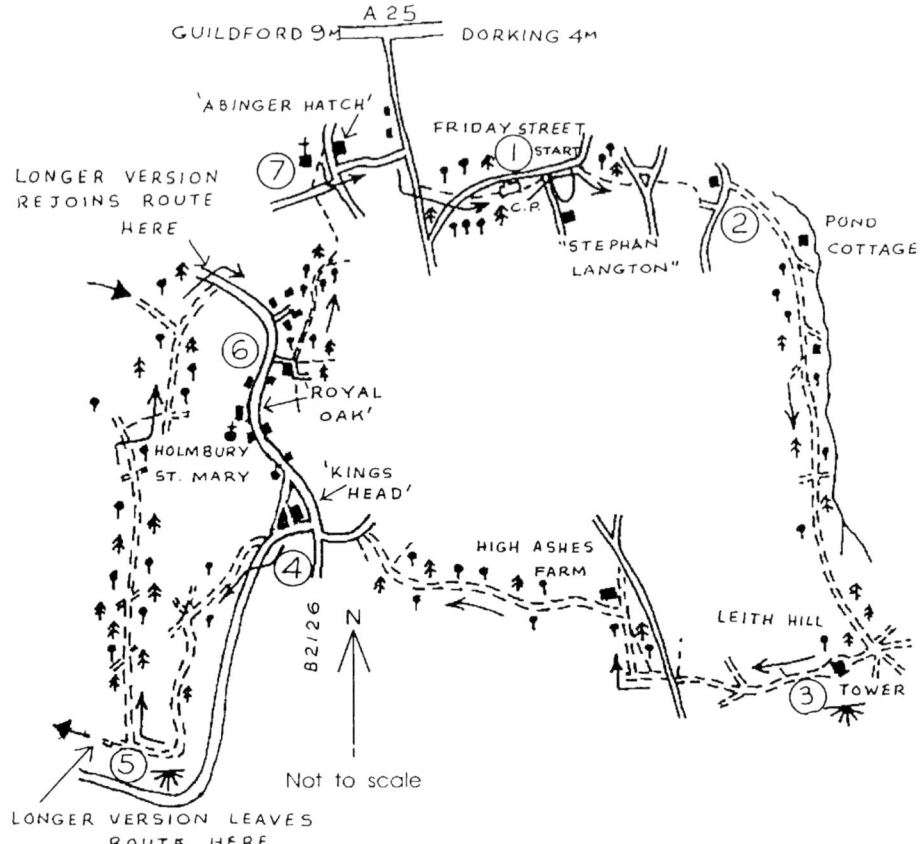

Length: 9 miles with alternatives of 6^1/$_2$ miles [fully described] and 13^1/$_2$ miles [outline only]. See map and end of paragraphs 3 and 4.

Maps: OS Landranger 187; Explorers 145 and 146.

Start: GR 127457 Surrey CC Friday Street [Free] car park. Travelling A25 from Guildford towards Dorking, turn right ^{1}/$_2$ mile beyond Wotton sign [Leith Hill, Friday Street] and in 1 mile turn sharp left. The car park is on the right in about ^{1}/$_4$ mile.

Transport: Tillingbourne, London & Country buses Guildford - Dorking to Holmbury St. Mary on B2126 [Felday Houses]. Join at 6.

Refreshments: Kings Head PH, Holmbury St. Mary; Abinger Hatch PH, Abinger Common; Stephan Langton Inn, Friday Street. Light refreshments served from Leith Hill Tower in summer [restricted opening in winter].

Introduction: This is a favourite walk because of the spectacular views offered both by the climb to Leith Hill and the walk along the Greensand Way to Holmbury Hill. It is best in autumn but enjoyable in all seasons; the variation in flora constantly provides something different. The tea bar in Leith Hill Tower serves excellent home made carrot cake.

THE WALK

1. Leave the car park by the NE corner and follow a footpath parallel to the road. Go down steps to join the road and continue forward to pass a lake on the right. Where the road bends left take a footpath on the right and walk at first steeply uphill, continuing forward to reach a minor road. Cross this and a second road and following a footpath sign descend via a gully to Broadmoor.

2. Turn left along the road to Triple Bar Riding Stables. Turn right along a track to pass a notice 'Private Road' to Pond Cottage and various houses. This is the Greensand Way [GW], a long distance footpath. Keep ahead and steadily uphill along Broadmoor Bottom for about $1^{1}/2$ miles to reach a junction of paths by Duke's Warren NT sign. Turn right and walk steeply uphill to Leith Hill Tower and superb views.

3. Leaving the tower on your right continue straight forward on the main track [GW] for $1/2$ mile to a road. Cross diagonally right to join a footpath ahead. In 200 yards reach a field corner on the left and take the second path right [GW marker] to go forward on a wide track to reach the drive to High Ashes Farm. Turn left along the drive and just before reaching the farm bear left [GW] downhill for about 1 mile to a road. Cross the road and turn left downhill to the T junction. [Care is needed on this narrow road.]Turn right and shortly left into Pitland Street.

To reach The Kings Head pub turn first right off Pitland Street.

Shorter version: instead of turning left into Pitland Street continue along the Horsham Road [B2126] for $1/2$ mile to reach a triangle of drives on the right, just past a house called Stagbury. Continue main route at 6.

4. Continue uphill along Pitland Street to pass a second road junction and reach a brick garage on the right. Turn sharp right onto a footpath which climbs steeply up to a cricket pitch. Keep straight ahead to a junction of five paths and here turn left onto the GW. At a fork in the path bear right and at the next fork bear left, keeping to the GW to reach the summit of Holmbury Hill.

Longer version: [NB this is an outline only. Use Explorer maps for more detail.] At Holmbury Hill continue on the GW, passing the summit of Pitch Hill then Ewhurst windmill, descending to a T-junction of minor roads. Take a bridlepath north, [Walk 4, Section 5 from line 3 describes this], then one north-east to reach Bently's, Hurtwood Centre, then a minor road to the centre of Peaslake. Here take a path from the roadway to the right of the village shop, in an easterly direction, to reach Holmbury Youth Hostel and in a short distance reach a bridleway crosspath. Turn left and walk down to the Horsham Road [B2126]. Turn right and follow directions at 6.

5. Leave the summit by the marked GW. In about 80 yards turn right to follow a grassy track to an open area and the junction of six tracks and a hostellers' metal seat. With your back to the seat you are faced with two tracks ahead. Take the lefthand track and follow this wide sandy ride in a northerly direction for 3/4 mile, ignoring four crossing tracks. Shortly after passing the fourth crossing track (a wide sandy track at right angles) look for a small track on the right into the trees. Follow this track, keeping ahead at the first junction, to reach a wide, sandy, downhill track [a fire break]. Turn left onto this track and in approximately 1/2 mile reach the road [B2126 Horsham Road] into Holmbury St. Mary. Turn right along this, following the footpath past a small housing estate, Felday Houses.

6. Turn left at a triangle of drives and take the path on the lefthand boundary of Tralee Lodge to reach a cross track and stiles. Turn left over a stile onto a broad grassy track, noting the power cables on your left, and follow this track for about 1/2 mile. Keep ahead, ignoring a path on the right, until overhead power lines are seen again. Look for a small track on the left away from these lines and follow this uphill to reach a stile into a field. Cross the field to a second stile and steps down to the road. Cross over and walk to the church which is worth a visit. The church was hit by a flying bomb during the war and restored in 1957.

7. Cross to the Abinger Hatch PH. Turn right and shortly left onto a minor road. Follow this road to the T junction and turn right. In 150 yards take a bridleway left along a gulley to join the road to Friday Street. Cross over and turn left along a track on the bank and so back to the car park.

11 Hydon Heath - Hambledon Church - Hascombe - Juniper Valley

Jean's walk

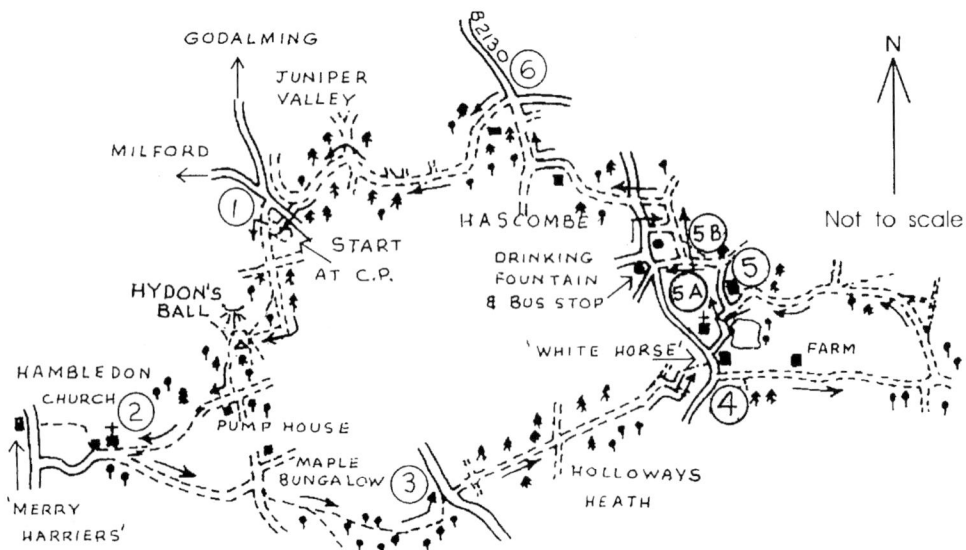

Length: 9 miles or 8 miles omitting section 4.

Maps: OS Landranger 186; Explorers 133, 134, 145.

Start: GR 979402 Hydon's Ball NT car park on minor road between Hascombe and Hydestile, from either Godalming (exit on B2130) or Milford (A3), 2 miles beyond railway station over cross roads.

Transport: Tillingbourne buses Godalming - Cranleigh via Hascombe. Join at 5A. Train to Milford station and walk 2 miles.

Refreshments: White Horse PH, Hascombe.

Introduction: This walk is best done in autumn for colour, and springtime and winter for thinner foliage and splendid views. Boots are advisable as some parts are muddy even in the summer.

THE WALK

1. From the car park walk back to the main track by which you arrived. Turn left up an incline, behind the NT Information Board, and ignore cross paths until you reach the top of the rise. Here take the path to the right to the top of the hill. This is known as Hydon's Ball and there is a long stone seat to the memory of Octavia Hill and fine views to the south and south east. From the seat bear right and take a broad path which soon bears left downhill. At a junction bear right onto a narrow track and continue downhill, ignoring any cross paths, to reach a bridleway where you turn sharp right with a brick pump house, Hydon's Ball booster station, on your left. The path crosses a plantation of coppiced chestnuts before bearing left to a metal kissing gate at the corner of an open field. Follow an obvious diagonal path across two fields to a wooden gate beside the churchyard. Hambledon Church is well worth a visit.

2. Continue on a bridleway to the left above the ancient lime kiln you may have noticed on arrival at the churchyard. Follow this for 1/2 mile to cross lanes with Maple Bungalow to your left. Turn right. Almost immediately take a tiny steep path up the bank on the left and, keeping high, continue along the undulating path near the top of a steep drop. Ignore a bridleway sign which soon points downhill and continue along the higher path through woodland. The path emerges to run along the righthand edge of two fields before re-entering woodland and descending to a small road.

3. Cross the road and take the bridlepath opposite, climbing quite steeply to a straight level track across Holloways Heath. Go straight ahead over a cross track until you descend into woodland and the bridleway bears left. Here follow the footpath with GW [Greensand Way] markers, first right and almost immediately left, and continue on a marked path to go steeply downhill left to a stile. Cross into a field and go forward over two more stiles to reach the road, B2130, and cross to the White Horse. This is a well known and busy pub, especially at weekends. It has a lovely garden and welcomes walkers.

Shorter version - turn left in front of the pub and walk along the lane, past the church and the pond, to School House. Continue at 5.

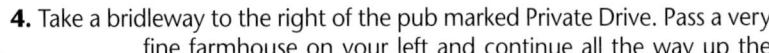

4. Take a bridleway to the right of the pub marked Private Drive. Pass a very fine farmhouse on your left and continue all the way up the cultivated valley to a col in the beech woods. The hill to your right is the site of an ancient fort. Turn left onto the path along the ridge, another marvellous viewpoint. Take time to gaze and ponder. Bear left where the broad path leaves the top of the ridge and follow down through woods on a spur between two valleys, to another attractive part of Hascombe village. Here you may wish to divert left a little to enjoy the peaceful green with seats around a pleasant pond or visit the church. You are also near to the White Horse PH once again. Retrace your steps to School House.

5. Pass in front of School House and other attractive houses and gardens. At the bridleway junction go left in front of a cottage. Continue along this track between hedges and look for a wooden chicane-style barrier on the left where the bridleway bears right. Here you have a choice.

5A - Take the short stretch of path to the road [and the bus stop] and note the impressive 1887 drinking fountain with a trough for animals, which is apparently still in use. From the fountain follow the village street to the right for a short distance to where the road starts bending and the footway finishes. Turn right into a signposted bridleway and go forward to rejoin the bridleway you left earlier, with a green metal gate, marked 'Stables', on the left.

Alternatively - 5B - continue by bearing right on the bridleway to reach a green metal gate ahead, marked 'Stables', and another bridleway coming in from the left.

Pass through the green metal gate which looks private when closed but is not. When this track bends to the right you turn left through a gate to reach the main road, B2130, through another green gate. Cross the road with great care to a bridleway directly opposite and follow steeply uphill through woods. At the top you reach a metalled lane with houses. Bear left for a short distance to a T junction and turn right to reach the road, the B2130 again!

6. Turn sharp left without entering the road, onto a wooded bridleway. In about $1/2$ mile ignore an open track forking right and continue forward to a steep descent into Juniper Valley. Take the second path left, with a footpath sign, which climbs gradually up a wide forest track until it comes close to the Hydestile/Hascombe road on the left, onto which there is a marked footpath exit. Cross the road and enter a very narrow path through herbage. This is a short cut to the well hidden car park where the walk began.

12 Dunsfold – Sussex Border Path – Plaistow

Julian's walk

Length: $9^{1}/_{4}$ miles.
Maps: OS Landranger 186; Explorers 134, 133.
Start: GR 013341 near Dunsfold. Limited parking in layby at start of track off Knightons Lane, leading to Upper Ifold Farm and Merrow Farm.

[To reach the start - Turn off B2130 to Dunsfold. Continue past the green then keep ahead over a crossroads with the Sun Inn on your right and past a turning left to Ifold and Horsham. Take the next turning left, Knightons Lane [signed to Knightons, Howicks and Upper Ifold] for 1 1/4 miles. Pass a turning off right and later a staggered crossroads and continue past a No Through Road sign. Pass Spunk's Cottage, Knightons and other houses on the left. After passing Woodlands go downhill and at the bottom immediately turn right to start the walk along a track marked Upper Ifold Farm and Merrow Farm.]

Transport: Bus to Plaistow and start at 5.

Refreshments: The Sun Inn, Plaistow.

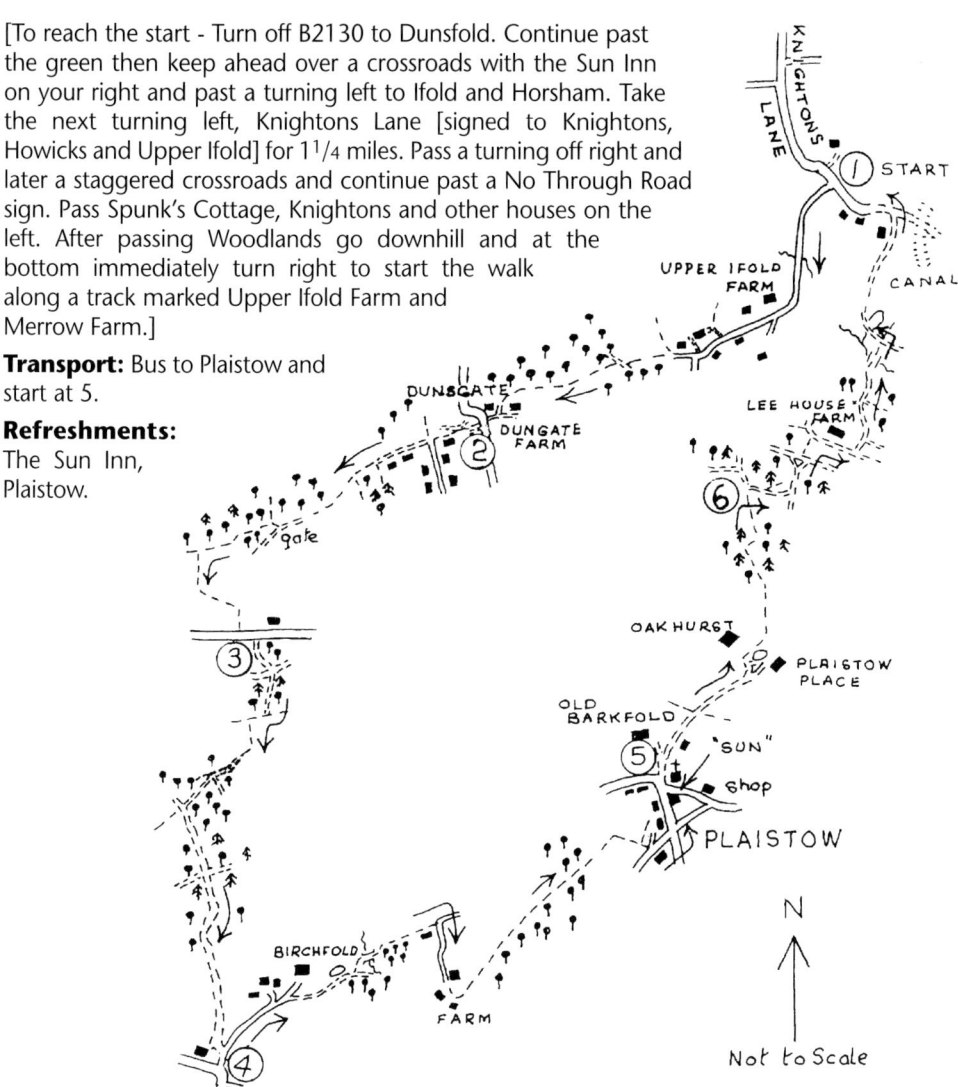

Introduction: This walk offers a chance to explore part of the Sussex Weald and includes quiet, open countryside with extensive views interspersed by woodland stretches. This is a good walk either in Summer when the trees afford welcome shade and it is less muddy than at other times of year, or in mid/late Spring when there is a carpet of bluebells and primroses in the woods. As this area is on wealden clay be prepared for a few muddy stretches in wet weather although the chosen route has sought to keep these to a minimum.

THE WALK

1. Follow a broad gravelled track with a bridleway fingerpost, and signed to Upper Ifold Farm. Continue as it becomes a metalled surface and crosses a stream, towards a farmhouse. Keep on past the entrance to Merrow Farm and a letter box on the left. Follow the track round to the left of farm buildings. Continue past The White House on the left and keep forward, ignoring a marker post for a path off right along a drive for deliveries to Upper Ifold House. Soon after this fork right and with a fence on your right keep forward along a broad track which now has a stony surface. Ignoring a field opening and a path sign on the right keep ahead on a narrower path through a strip of woodland. As this opens out into a larger area of woodland bear left, slightly uphill, using the banktop path if the main track is muddy. Reach a T junction with a forest track. Turn right and almost immediately peel off left on a grassy track by a sign 'Riding by Permit Only'. Follow this path through the trees and continue as it passes a field on the left. As you near a house the path bears left up a slope to a gateway and emerges onto a drive with a fingerpost ahead signing the Sussex Border Path [SBP]. Turn right by this out to a road beside a house, Dunsgate. The Border Path is a 150 mile route around the inland county border and the Sussex Martlet emblem appears on the badge of Sussex County Cricket Club and on the County Coat of Arms.

2. Cross the road to Primrose View and follow the SBP along a signed path to the right of the drive. This narrow path soon merges with a broader one coming in from the right but shortly bears left onto a narrower track again, alongside gardens. Keep forward over a roadway, ignoring a path off right, and follow a broad gravelled track. Continue between houses and keep forward onto a grassy fenced track between gardens leading into a woodland path. Follow the bridleway, passing a fingerpost and ignoring paths off left, until you reach a small gate into a field. Keep ahead through the gate, still on the SBP, through two fields with woodland to your right. There are wide open views here with Bexley Hill ahead distinguished by it's radio mast. Come through a gate [usually open] onto a grassy track with a fenced field to the left and still with woodland right. At a second farm gate ahead marked Private turn right into the wood by a SBP fingerpost. Turn immediately left along the edge of the wood still following the SBP. Soon after crossing a stream on a footbridge you pass a field on the left with a large painted corrugated iron barn in the corner. Watch for a stile on the left in the corner of the next field. Cross a plank bridge and the stile into this field and turn right along the edge. At the field corner, by a fingerpost, turn left, leaving the SBP. Walk down the field edge with a fence on your right, enjoying the open views. Go through a field gate and turn left in the next field with a hedge on your left. At the next corner turn right, still with a hedge on your left, to reach a small metal gate leading out to a road.

3. Turn left along the road and in about 100 yards, just past a field entrance, turn right by a bridleway sign into woodland. As you turn there is a good view of Black Down across the fields to your right. This woodland track soon bears left going up a rise through pine woods with fields glimpsed over to your right. Reach a junction of paths. Turn right then immediately fork left [ignore right fork to fields and a stile] onto a grassy and rather overgrown track. This goes along the edge of woodland with fields over to the right. Reach a small gate leading into a field by a fingerpost. In the field turn right to the corner then turn left by another fingerpost, walking along the edge of the same field with a hedge on your right. Reach a metal gate at the corner of woodland. There are good views again towards Black Down ahead and to the right. Go through the gate and continue along the edge of a wood with fields to the right. Where the woodland opens out to a partly cleared area with young oaks, ignore a narrower path which continues beside the field and a broad track which turns off left alongside the denser woodland, and bear slightly left onto a central path. This central path, sometimes rather overgrown, crosses the more open woodland and bears gradually left to the far corner then leads out to a junction with a crossing bridleway and a four-way fingerpost. Again there are good views ahead, over a small gate, across the fields to Black Down. Turn left here along the bridleway, now with a field on your right. Ignore a turning off left and follow a broad track through mixed woodland. Reach a large crossing track with a two-way fingerpost on the left and keep ahead. Muddy stretches can be avoided by walking through the woods on either side. Reach a broken down gate, with a bench mark on the gatepost, where a track goes off left, and here swing right in line with a bridleway fingerpost. There are now fields on your left and soon also on the right. This track can become rather overgrown but is one of the old broad 'green lanes' running through Sussex. Follow this and towards the end keep left, avoiding a branch right with overhead power lines, to reach a small surfaced lane.

4. Turn left along the lane for 300 yards and reach farm buildings ahead at a junction of drives. Bear round to the right, leaving Chilsfold Farm on the left, to join a gravel track. Just before the entrance to Birchfold turn right by a fingerpost onto a broad grassy path and keep to this fenced track which later swings left heading down towards woodland. Pass a pond with water lillies on the left and then descend into woodland. At a junction with a fingerpost turn left and follow a path down to cross a stout footbridge. Go through a small gate and turn left for about 25 yards then turn right uphill following the righthand field edge. Keep forward to a metal gate and enter a grass track with a corrugated barn on the right and soon meet a surfaced farm drive. Turn right and follow the drive to reach farm buildings. Pass to the right of the farmhouse and into a yard with traditional old barns. Bear round to the left to emerge into an open field. Head for the far corner where the left and right hedge converge and go through the opening into another field. Bear right to a gate. Continue through the gate keeping ahead along the righthand edge of the next three fields. At the far end of the third field head down to a small gate-cum-stile in the corner. Cross this to follow a small woodland path beside a stream on the right. Keep forward where another path joins from the left, crossing a plank bridge over the stream and then rising gently. Come out with a clearing to your left and keep ahead over a stile by a fingerpost into a field. Walk straight up the field, in line with the fingerpost, where the spire of Plaistow Church comes into view ahead of you. Make for a fingerpost on the outer corner of the hedge and turn right along the field edge with the hedge on your left. Follow the hedge round to the left, passing a stile and footbridge on the left, and keep round to go over a stile onto a gravel drive. From here turn right and immediately left up the lane to a crossroads. Turn left towards the church and find The Sun Inn on the right. [There is a Village Stores beyond the cricket ground, reached by continuing forward at the crossroads - see map.]

5. Beyond The Sun Inn and a lane to the right, where the road swings left, keep forward onto a rough track with the church immediately on your right. Pass a small bungalow, The Parsonage, and follow the track as it swings right through a gate by the entrance to Old Barkfold on the left. As the ground rises there are splendid views to the right with the South Downs in the far distance. The track leads up beside farm buildings and towards a large house, Plaistow Place, ahead. Before reaching this house turn left onto a drive leading to another attractive tilehung house. Just before the gate to this turn through the second gate on the right by a fingerpost. Follow the righthand edge of a field forming part of the gardens to the house and keep right round to the far corner to go over a stile. Continue forward along the righthand field edge,

past an opening to the right, to the end of the field and a stile in the far corner. Over this keep ahead on a woodland path and reach a two-way fingerpost by a T junction in front of a small bank. Turn right. In about 50 yards reach another fingerpost and turn left. Descend gently and at the bottom of the slope leave the wood and keep forward over a scrub area. Re-enter woodland by a fingerpost and a marker post for the Sussex Border Path [SBP].

6. Turn right here onto the SBP and at a fork keep right to reach a broad track at a marker post. Turn left to a junction with a broad crossing track and keep straight ahead to a grassy path with a marker post indicating a continuation of the SBP. Soon reach another path junction with a field ahead and here turn right, still following the SBP, with the field on your left. Join a broad gravel track by the entrance to Lee House Farm. Keep ahead for 50 yards then turn left onto a signposted path, leaving the SBP. Ignore all turnings off right and keep along the track passing a house and field then farm buildings on your left. Ignore a further track off right and continue forward until you reach a gate leading into a field. Go straight across the field to find a broad bridge over a stream. In the next field bear slightly left and go up the slope to a gate. Here turn left and go down the slope again along the edge of the same field [thus keeping to the definitive path line] and come to another gate with a large pond on the right. Go forward past the pond into woodland alongside a fence on your right. Keep to the path which gradually bears round to the right and continues some way through the woodland before coming alongside a high wire fence as you approach a house on the left. Keep round by the fence with the bed of the old Wey and Arun canal on your right and reach a broad gravel drive. Turn left down this passing the entrance to the house, Sydney Court, and keep along the track which becomes a metalled lane and passes Old Knightons and Old Knightons Cottage then descends to reach the starting point.

13 Hindhead – Marley Common – Hammer – Waggoners Wells

Joy's Walk

Length: 12^1/$_2$ miles.

Maps: OS Landranger 186; Explorer 133.

Start: GR 891357 National Trust car park at the Punchbowl, Hindhead, off A3.

Transport: Stagecoach buses to Hindhead crossroads from Haslemere; Godalming via Chiddingfold; or Bordon.

Refreshments: The Mill Tavern, Shottermill; Prince of Wales PH, Hammer; Little Chef on A3, Bramshott Common area; Hillcrest Cafe at start/finish of walk.

Introduction: This is one of my favourite walks in Surrey. There are lots of ups and downs and new viewpoints keep appearing as we circle around. There are plenty of bilberries and blackberries in season and a good selection of wild flowers. It's an 'all season walk' but I like it best in the winter months with a covering of snow or a heavy frost; it's a brisk trot round but exhilarating.

'Progress' has changed the route in two places. The railway is now too busy to recommend crossing the line at Hammer; the fast, new trains are very quiet and give little warning of their approach. The A3 above Hammer now has crash barriers both sides of the central reservation with no gaps and, as this is not a good place for trip hurdles, I've found a safer place to cross.

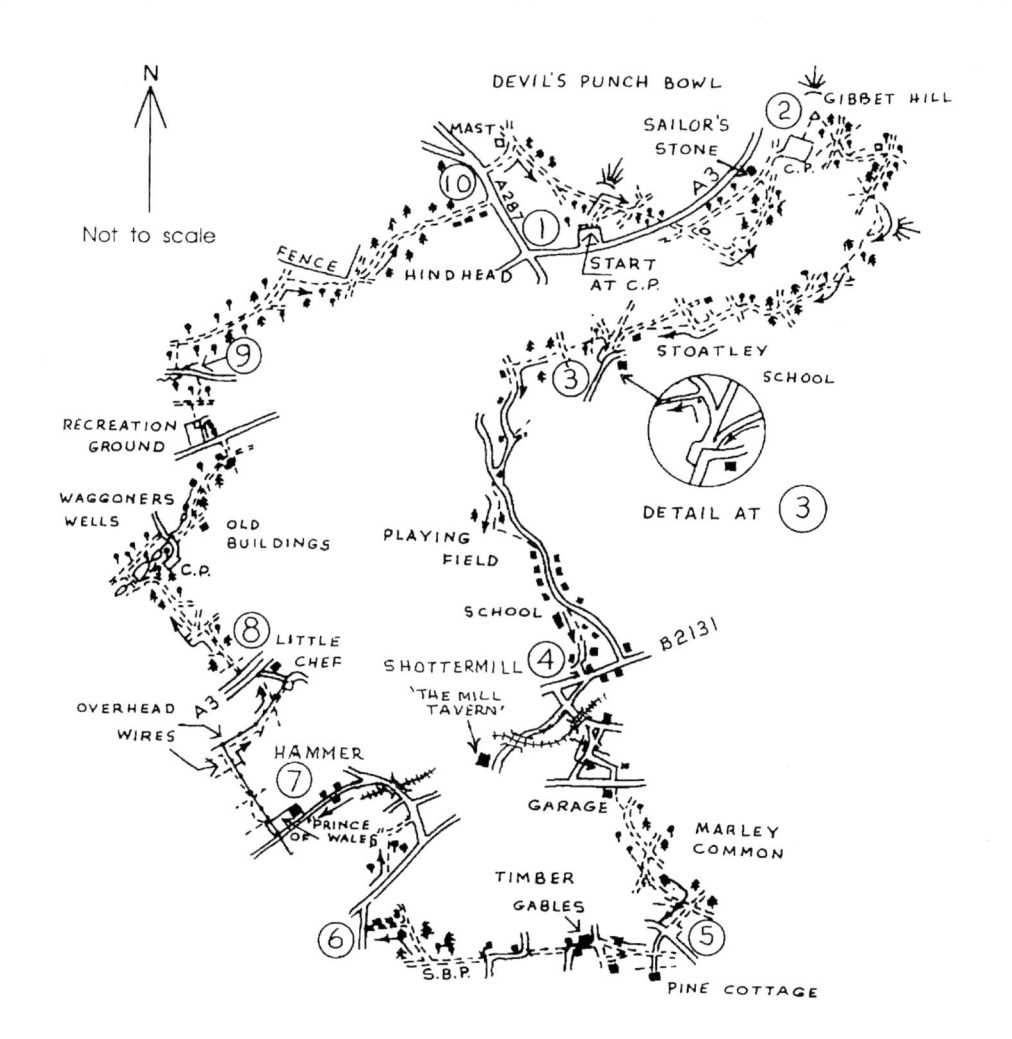

THE WALK

1. Take the path under the wooden arch, with the cafe on your left, and bear round to the right passing the NT Information Board. Go forward then fork left to go down steps to the edge of the Punch Bowl with grand views of Sugarloaf Hill and the North Downs. Turn right, ignore the first path on the right and just after another broad path joins from the right, leave the main path before reaching a gate and go ahead on a path to the A3. Carefully cross to the bridleway opposite by the NT Hindhead Common sign. Pass straight over at a crosstrack keeping the remains of a pond on your left. Follow the path through a clearing, with views of the South Downs to your right, and into woods. Ignore paths off right to reach a small car park [or rubbish tip!]. Exit through bars and keep straight on, continuing over a crossing track. After 40/50 yards take a small track on the left to the Sailor's Stone [complete with curse] with grand views over the A3 down into the Punch Bowl. Turn right up the old Portsmouth coach road. At a junction go right into a larger car park and keeping trees on your left make for the

37

'trig point' on Gibbet Hill. There are views of the North Downs and Hascombe Hill in front of you and the diagram on top of the trig point identifies the hills. Bilberries abound here.

2. Take a narrow path forward half right [E] towards East Grinstead, which goes into the woods and downhill. Passing through bars at a path junction take the third on the left going more or less straight on, first uphill then down. At a junction with a bridleway keep to the right, still downhill. Watch for the base of a Temple on the left. Keep straight on to reach Hurthill Copse at the eastern edge of the hill. At the base of a seat on the left of a junction of paths, take the first on the right [SSW] leading past chestnut woods with views over Grayswood glimpsed to the left. Continue uphill to a five path junction and take the second track to the left [S], still uphill. At the top of the rise take a small path left leading to a seat and viewpoint over the South Downs. This small track leads back to the main path. Here turn left, gently downhill, passing an old iron gate and posts. Keep on winding downhill and at a fork take the righthand path [SW] still downhill. At the next crossing track, with NT marker post and arrows, turn right [W] and cross over two junctions with further NT marker posts, into trees. The path swings to the right going downhill fairly steeply. At the bottom by some tall beeches go over a track and straight on along a fenced track over a stream. Ignoring a track on the right carry on uphill round the bend to the right, soon passing Coombeswell NT sign on the left. Take a path immediately on the left uphill with later a hedge on the left. On reaching a garden shed on the left join the main bridleway and turn left uphill passing houses on your left. Pass Quartermaine School and Royal School on the left. At the road end, with Royal School Stoatley on the left, take the main path right for ten paces then a left fork [N] for twelve paces then turn again left down a small path by a rowan tree.

3. Go downhill through woods, ignore a small cross path, and keep winding downhill. At a larger crossing track, the Greensand Way, go straight over and downhill through bracken to the bottom of Polecat Valley. Turn left into a lane and follow this to the road. Turn left for about twenty paces then right up a bank by beeches, turning left onto a small path above the road. Follow this round into tall pine trees. At a field on the left [sometimes used for football and sports days] turn down the bank onto it. Follow the hedge round on the left to join a road just before the first house on the right. Turn right along the pavement and follow the road to Shottermill School and a post box and telephone box. Take a footpath by the playground [cycling sign] going uphill between fences to metal bars. Reach a road and pass the Adult Education Centre and clinic. Where the road goes right keep straight on down a small road to reach a main road [B2131] at The Tasty, a Chinese take-away.

4. Cross the road to go right and down Liphook Road opposite, to traffic lights. [To reach The Mill Tavern keep straight on at the lights. It is just beyond the railway bridge on the right. Retrace your steps to the traffic lights.] Turn left down Sturt Road and go under the railway bridge. At Number One, Sickle Mill House, turn right across the road onto a track and keep forward over a narrow, brick pedestrian bridge and on to a road. Go forward then left up next road, swinging right by Camelsdale School. At a crossing road cross to the left to the end of a garage complex, then go right uphill on a footpath. After 30 yards turn left up a sandy bank to join the main track and turn right uphill. At a crossing track at the top of the rise, after about 500 yards, turn right. At a footpath sign at a fork go left and keep straight on, ignoring right turns, to a six path junction. Take the second right, the Sussex Border Path [SBP], passing a new enclosure of trees on the right, and go through a car park to a road.

5. Cross the road and go down a drive opposite to Pine Cottage. At a crossing track before a house turn right [W]. Just before the next house on the left, fork slightly to the right, passing a SBP sign. Join the road at a bend, turn left on it, passing Timber Gables on your right, and when the road goes left keep straight ahead on a path. Follow SBP signs to the next road. Turn left at road and when this goes left, keep straight on to the second set of signposts by a house. Turn right [NW] leaving the SBP. Ignoring side paths and a crossing one, keep straight on downhill, passing an old gatepost, to enter chestnut coppices. After $1/2$ mile or a little more, at a fork before bungalows and a large oak and a chestnut, go left round the edge of a housing estate to reach a road at a gate.

6. Turn right on the road to a T junction, passing a telephone box on the right. Turn right, cross over and take a footpath downhill on the right of the cemetery. At the bottom, with a football field on the left, turn right onto a stony track. After passing cottages follow a fence down on the left to a road. Turn left on the road, pass Moor Road, and cross the railway into Hampshire and Hammer Vale. Go over streams with Pophole Iron Works on your right. Keep left at Sandy Lane and continue through the hamlet to the Prince of Wales, a Gales pub. Ramblers are welcome here as long as muddy boots are covered, but beware, no food after 2.00pm.

7. Refreshed, with the saloon bar door behind you, go to the far righthand end of the car park and turn right uphill near the overhead wires. At cross tracks keep on uphill still following overhead wires. At a junction of paths and overhead wires, at the top of the hill, go right. Later swing left with the path and wires, ignoring a path to the right. After post 933 and before the next one, look for a path on the left by a hedge and follow this to the road by a Little Chef. Turn left here and cross the A3, with care, to a fingerpost left of a crossing point on the north-bound road.

8. Go down steps [NW] and downhill to a crossing track at the bottom. Go straight ahead uphill where there is heather in all directions in season, and at a second crossing track on the brow of the hill, by an MOD notice and NT Bramshott Common sign, turn left for about 100 yards. At a clearing and widening of track turn right downhill on a broad grass track. Ignore the track to the right and keep downhill. At a fingerpost keep on to reach the lake at Waggoners Wells. Turn left, then right across the end of the lake. The house down the path to the left was once a tea shop known to cyclists and walkers all over the county: alas, now it's an ordinary house! So turn right to follow the lakeside and look out for the huge carp. Keep straight on at the next lake to meet a small road at a stream. Go to the right over this and a little before the road bears right into a car park, take the bridleway to the left uphill for about 50 yards and with an old building on your right, turn half left forward over a bank. Small ponds now appear. Go downhill to these keeping them on your left and keep ahead to reach the waterworks at Stoney Bottom. Keep straight on passing houses on your left. At crossing tracks, Kingswood Ruffs is on the right, turn left and go steeply uphill to a road. Cross this and go left along the pavement. At the recreation ground turn right up Beech Hanger Road, pass tennis courts on your right, then turn left into the cricket ground. Keep to the right through the car park, passing football goals and cricket nets. Turn right at the end of the fields, cross a track and go left into woods at a fingerpost. Proceed downhill, it is steep in places, to reach a road.

9. Turn left on the road down to a stream. Cross this, pass 'Hampshire - Grayshott' sign and immediately turn right uphill 90° through trees to join a crossing track. Turn right, still uphill. Keep to the main track, ignoring paths either side, [the Golden Valley is on your left] to almost the top of the rise where a wire fence can be seen ahead. Turn right at a waymark post on the left. The path winds towards the fence and joins it at a corner on your left. Keep on to a clearing and take the third path on the right [E] going straight on. The path wanders through the wood, slightly uphill. After ¾ mile or so houses start to appear off to your right. Follow the path to a road.

10. At the road turn left along the grass verge of the Hindhead/Farnham road [A287]. Just after a blue 'Narrow Bridge' sign cross the road to go up a bridleway to High Combe Pines to the right of the Guide Dogs for the Blind Association. This swings left at Gorse Hill. Go by the mast on the left and at once turn right at a junction of paths along the top of the Devil's Punch Bowl. Through gaps in the trees you can again see Sugarloaf Hill on your left. Pass a cottage on your right. Ignore paths off either side until you get back to your first view of Sugarloaf Hill. Then go right up sandy steps and back to the car park. The cafe does a good cup of tea and a fine all day breakfast.

14 Hindhead – Gibbet Hill - Thursley – Hankley Common – Devil's Punch Bowl

Norman and Jeverley's walk

Length: 10 or 12 miles with an extension to The Hankley PH.

Maps: OS Landranger 186; Explorers 133, 145.

Start: GR 891357 National Trust car park at the Punchbowl, Hindhead, on A3.

Transport: Stagecoach buses to Hindhead crossroads from Haslemere; Godalming via Chiddingfold; and Bordon.

Refreshments: The Hankley PH, Hankley Common / Tilford; The Three Horseshoes PH, Thursley; Hillcrest Cafe, Hindhead at the start / finish of the walk.

Introduction: This is one of the earliest walks which we led for the Godalming and Haslemere group and one which was a favourite family walk when the children were young. It follows the Greensand Way and the old Portsmouth coach road between Hindhead and Thursley, with a touch of local history added by the story of an unknown sailor who was robbed and murdered near Gibbet Hill. His murderers were later hung on the gibbet. There is a memorial stone to the sailor, inscribed with the story, in Thursley churchyard. The route is mostly on high ground over well drained greensand heathlands, with extensive views throughout. However, where the spring line has eroded the overlying rock to form the punchbowl, the ground may be muddy.

THE WALK

1. Proceed north through the left of the two wooden archways onto a footpath which bears right, then go straight through small posts [NE] along a wide footpath. Bear left at a V fork of paths. A view of the Punch Bowl is ahead. Walk down the wide steps to the viewpoint where Sugarloaf Hill can be seen directly ahead to the east of the Punch Bowl. Turn sharp right and follow a footpath through trees. After 200 yards, just after merging with a broad path from the right, bear right onto a narrow path towards the A3. Note pale blue direction arrows on a small post on the left. Cross the A3 to a bridleway directly opposite. At the first crossing path turn sharp left into the old Portsmouth coach road, now a wide track. Walk straight ahead towards Gibbet Hill passing, after about 1/4 mile, the 'Sailor's Stone' with a viewpoint. An unknown sailor was murdered very close to this site on 24th September 1786 by three villains who had followed him from the old Red Lion pub at Thursley, to get his money. Walk straight ahead for about 80 yards to a car park sign, take a right fork then bear left walking up to the trig point on top of Gibbet Hill. The viewpoint identifies places looking across the Weald with the Surrey Hills in the distance. A Celtic Cross of Light marks the site of the gibbet where the three villains and other murderers, highwaymen etc. were hanged.

2. From the trig point turn left and take the footpath on the right, slightly in front of the cross, going downhill into the wood. This is part of the Greensand Way [GW]. At the footpath junction with a GW sign, go through a wooden horse rider's barrier then turn left. Walk about 45 yards then turn right to rejoin the old coach road. At a footpath fork, 1/2 mile along this stony path, keep to the main path ignoring the path on the left. Continue along this path to where it joins the A3.

3. Cross over the A3 to a path opposite which is going north, nearly parallel with the A3. You are still on the Greensand Way. Proceed through a gate beside a cattle grid, turn sharp left and go up to the top of Sugarloaf Hill and a viewpoint. Follow the footpath going directly across and downhill, ignoring all side paths, to rejoin the GW. Bearing left on this broad path, which is still part of the old coach road, and ignoring side paths, continue until you reach a broad crossing path and a post on the left with four red arrows on top.

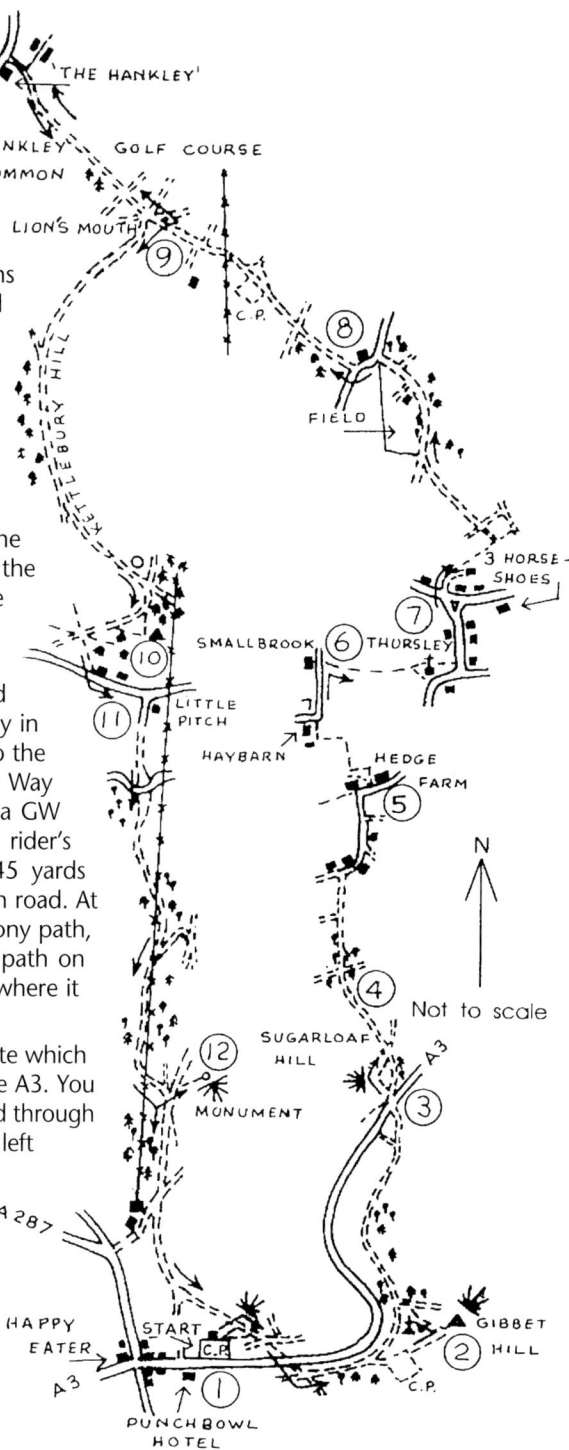

41

4. Walk straight ahead and after about 200 yards go through a gate beside a cattle grid, near a GW signpost. Continue straight ahead on a wider path, passing the entrance to Cowdray Cross House on the left, to the junction of a path and a paved road. Bear right onto the road, still on the GW, passing a postbox and Upper Highfield Farm and Cottage on the right. Follow the road for 350 yards to where it bends to the right with Hedge Farm House on the left. After 20 yards turn sharp left through a large wooden gate with a footpath sign on the left in a hedge and a name board for Hedge Farm.

5. Walk on about 10 yards and into a narrow path on the extreme right with a yellow arrow on a post. Ignore paths on the left and follow the fenced footpath over three stiles and around farm fields. At the third stile carry straight on, with the hedge on your left, to the corner ahead. Then go over a fourth stile onto a path with fences on the right and left. Turn right between hedges, passing Haybarn, to reach a paved lane and carry on to Small Brook Farm on the left.

6. Turn sharp right at a footpath sign with a GW yellow arrow. Go up a small bank and over a stile into a field. Look for Thursley church spire diagonally over the field and walk towards it to a stile in the far corner. Cross the stile and follow a path over further stiles into the graveyard of Thursley church. The murdered sailor's grave is marked by a very large stone standing by itself to the left of the path and depicts the 'barborous act' in relief. Leave the graveyard over a stone stile into the roadway, turning left along the road to reach Thursley / Thors Lee village sign set on a triangular patch of grass. [The Three Horseshoes PH is to the right.]

7. Take the left fork, The Street, and cross the main road into a driveway to the right of a telephone box directly opposite. A bridleway sign is hidden in the hedge on the left. Follow the bends in the path, beside houses on the right, for a short distance to a garage ahead with a narrow path on the left. Take this path to a junction then turn sharp left at the signpost to a further path junction with a 'permissive bridleway' sign. Go straight ahead on a very sandy path. Follow bends in the path soon reaching fields on the left and passing two or three posts at intervals with blue HR arrows on top. At a further path junction take the lefthand fork, beside a post with a blue arrow, to reach another path fork. Take the lefthand path to a farm track. Bear right and go straight ahead to join a main road. Truxford Riding Centre noticeboard can be seen to the left across the road.

8. Turn sharp left then cross over the road, near chevrons, into an MoD tarmac road. Follow this, passing a car park, and go over the hill down to a clearing where the road turns left. Look for a post marked 101 on the right, with MoD buildings on the left. Leave the tarmac road along 101 [NW]. The path is very sandy. Follow track 101 to a six path junction and clearing. An un-numbered marker post is ahead with fences on the left enclosing MoD property.

To continue main route see 9.

To make the diversion to The Hankley PH walk over the clearing, bearing right to a marker post for track 101 on the left. Walk straight on, ignoring paths to the left, to reach Hankley Common golf course. Walk straight across path junctions, still on path 101, passing between faded pink painted posts, and continue ahead on 101 over the golf course. Ignore paths crossing the course to eventually reach a caravan park on the left. Walk straight ahead, passing the Golf Club House and car park on the right, to join a paved road left leading to the main Tilford Road with The Hankley pub on the left corner. To rejoin the main route return down the paved road and re-cross the golf course walking the same path in reverse, to the large clearing and junction of paths at the end of section 8. Regain the main route by turning right uphill with the wire fence on your left, as described at the beginning of section 9.

9. Turn left, keeping the wire fence to your left, and climb uphill on a wide sandy path for about 120 yards, to the edge of 'Lion's Mouth'. There is a lovely panoramic view here. Turn right, with a path 108 post on the right, along the top of Kettlebury Hill and continue for 1³/₄ miles, ignoring tracks joining or crossing it. All along this path it is worth stopping to look at the views. Power lines can sometimes be seen through the trees ahead but before reaching them there is a junction of paths on the edge of woodland. Turn right, with the trees to your left, following bends in the path, again ignoring tracks to left and right, and go uphill to a Y junction of paths. Take the left fork more steeply uphill to the trig point on top of Kettlebury Hill, where there are extensive views.

10. Bear right down the main footpath. Take a left fork and walk about 70 yards to a junction of paths. Turn sharp left here to reach the main road. Turn left along the road, passing a second set of houses called Silver Birches and Springs on the left, to reach a junction with arrows on a post on the left and a house called Little Pitch on the right.

11. Turn right into a track. A fingerpost is hidden in a holly hedge on the right. Walk slightly uphill, ignoring farm tracks on the right of the path, through a gully and trees to a paved road. Cross over the road to a path opposite with a bridleway sign on the right. Follow the path which turns into a narrow gully and comes to a National Trust sign on the left. At this point pylons on the left change to the right side of the path as you walk under the cables. Walk on to a footpath junction where there is a post with three blue arrows on your left, but carry straight on along the path with the pylons still on your right. The path gradually rises towards the top of the Punch Bowl and eventually merges with a broad crossing track. Turn left to a footpath fork and bear right to a viewpoint and a wooden seat with nearby a quite well known memorial stone to the Robertson Brothers, killed in World War I.

12. Retrace your steps to the previous fork and the junction with the main footpath. Bear left and continue uphill to where a path forks left. Ignore this left fork, keeping to the main track with glimpses on the left to the far side of the Punch Bowl and beyond. Carry on along the path until a square, metal high vehicle barrier is reached. Just after this, at a junction of paths, turn left opposite the gates of an electricity sub-station. Walk along the footpath for about 850 yards until the viewpoint at the foot of the wide steps is reached. Turn right up the steps and retrace the short distance to the car park.

15 Frensham Ponds – River Wey – Shortfield Common – Tilford

Denis and Susan's walk

Length: 10¹/₂ miles and shorter versions of 6 or 4¹/₂ miles.
Maps: OS Landranger 186; Explorer 145.

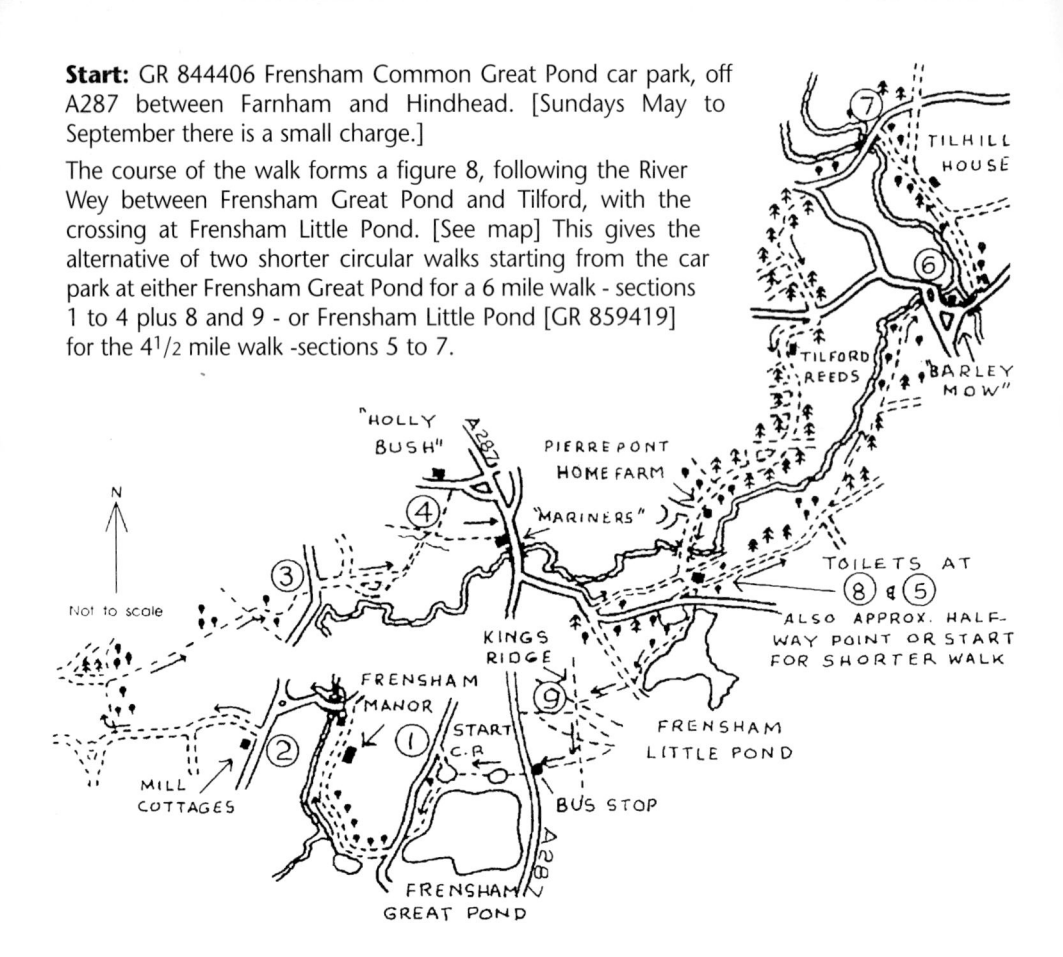

Start: GR 844406 Frensham Common Great Pond car park, off A287 between Farnham and Hindhead. [Sundays May to September there is a small charge.]

The course of the walk forms a figure 8, following the River Wey between Frensham Great Pond and Tilford, with the crossing at Frensham Little Pond. [See map] This gives the alternative of two shorter circular walks starting from the car park at either Frensham Great Pond for a 6 mile walk - sections 1 to 4 plus 8 and 9 - or Frensham Little Pond [GR 859419] for the 4^1/$_2$ mile walk -sections 5 to 7.

Transport: Stagecoach buses Aldershot - Haslemere passing Frensham Great Pond on A287 [near start / end of 9 - see map] and Shortfield Common [join at 4]: or Hindhead - Elstead, Liphook - Farnham via Tilford [join at 6].

Refreshments: The Holly Bush PH, Shortfield Common; The Mariners PH, Millbridge; The Barley Mow PH, Tilford. Rangers Office with an Information Centre, a small shop and toilet facilities at start.

Introduction: This walk lies in the south west corner of Surrey, a particularly pretty part of the county with a varied landscape, largely due to a wide band of sandstone. This gives rise to rolling hills with extensive views and winding rivers at their base, woodlands of mixed deciduous and coniferous trees, and open heathland often with boggy patches or open water where drainage is poor. We like this walk because it offers a taste of all these features: the sandy tracks assure walking free of mud even in wet weather and mid-winter; part of it is through an Area of Outstanding Natural Beauty which includes a Nature Reserve; and it can be split into two shorter walks. Frensham Great Pond and Frensham Little Pond are artificial lakes and were excavated in the 13th century to provide fish for the Bishop of Winchester's estate. The heathland around them is rich in wildlife, acting as a sanctuary for many rare species of birds, insects, spiders, reptiles and mammals, as well as plants. This area has been managed as a Country Park since 1971. However, this popular area on both si[des of the] [A287] and also around both ponds, suffers badly from erosion, so the cours[e] may occasionally be changed but usually by only a few yards. Walkers are requ[ested to keep] on the paths and not to walk across the heather, to minimize the effects of erosion [on this rare] and very special habitat. Heathland is internationally endangered, and with almo[st 20% of the] world total in the United Kingdom, this lovely area of Surrey is especially precious.

THE WALK

1. Facing the lake, turn right and take the track at the far end of the car park. With the lake on the left follow the track along the lake edge to the road. Turn left at the road for a short distance round the end of the lake to a bridleway on the right, immediately before a sunken stream outlet from the lake. Follow the bridleway past a pond on the left, through trees and beside the river Wey [south branch] to exit past Frensham Manor and onto a road at The Mill House. Turn left and cross the bridge over the river, leaning over the old bargate-stone wall to watch the mill-race for a few minutes. Continue to a T junction on the Tilford / Farnham road and turn left onto a grassy bank across the road for a short distance to a bridleway on the right immediately before Mill Cottages.

2. Follow the bridleway between fields for about 1/2 mile to a waymarked stile on the right. Over the stile cross a field for a short distance to the corner of a wood and another waymarked stile. Follow the footpath steeply uphill through the wood to a crossing trail at the top. Turn right and follow this wide track through the wood and into a field with a line of trees on the right. Continue along the ridge, enjoying the extensive views on both sides, to the corner of the field with a wood ahead. Here the farm track bends left, but go forward on a footpath which winds through the wood, with a carpet of bluebells in the spring. Emerge over a stile into an open field and turn left beside the hedge for about 80 yards to another wood ahead. Ignoring the stile on the left and the footpath going downhill right, enter the wood over a stile slightly left. Emerge from the wood into a field with a slight slope upward and turn right along the field edge, curving round to a stile at the rear of a large house. Across a wide valley to the left is a magnificent view of the lovely old buildings of Frensham Heights School. Over the stile follow the footpath through a wicket gate and along the left side of the school drive, under trees, to the end of the drive and then down to a road.

3. Cross the road to go down the 'No Through Road' past The Malt House. The road soon becomes a waymarked track. Bear left, ignoring the footpath and paved drive on the right. At the red-brick house just ahead, turn left and follow the sunken footpath between banks and over a small bridge crossing a stream. Go ahead up the grassy slope for a few yards then turn right along the boundary fence of the sports ground at Shortfield Common. [Just here there is a stile to a footpath across the sports ground, leading to a road and The Holly Bush PH.]

4. Follow the boundary fence on the field side to the corner of the sports ground, then go over a stile and steeply downhill for a few yards on a footpath which exits at the road to Farnham [A287] beside The Mariners PH. Turn right at the road, crossing the bridge over the river Wey, south branch. After a short distance turn left at The Old Post House and follow a lane towards Frensham Little Pond. The lane is narrow, with no side pavement, so beware of passing traffic. Round a sharp bend to the right,

45

down bridleway P2, opposite a riding school field. Follow the bridleway through woods to a bridleway T junction and turn right to Toilets. Frensham Little Pond is just ahead across a paved track.

Shorter versions: the route of 6 miles can be taken here, returning to Great Pond by continuing at 8; or, with a start from the Frensham Little Pond car park at this point, the route of $4^{1}/_{2}$ miles to Tilford and back following sections 5 - 7.

5. Just past the Toilets turn left and follow bridleway 522. After about $^{1}/_{2}$ mile cross over a waymarked stile on the left and follow the footpath through the wood. This becomes a stony track passing a farm and then a house on the left. Immediately past the driveway to the house, take the waymarked footpath on the left, which continues through woodland, soon with the river Wey, southern branch, on the left. The river bank along here, with a wooden seat provided at one point, makes a pleasant resting place. Leaving the river, go through a wicket gate and follow the path alongside a tree nursery, exiting at the road by Tilford Green. Keeping to the left of the sloping green, admire the Tilford Oak, recorded by Cobbett during his travels. A few yards further on is the Barley Mow pub, providing an ideal halfway stop for refreshments after the first 6 miles, and perhaps, in the summer, a rest to watch a cricket match.

6. A few yards past the pub the river Wey is crossed by an old stone bridge, with a ford below where the water is shallow, providing a favourite bathing place for children in the summer. The river at Tilford is formed by the junction of the north and south branches just above the bridge. Cross the bridge and turn left onto the bridleway immediately before the village stores, with the north branch of the river in the valley on the left. The bridleway leads uphill to a paved track. Continue left past Tilhill House and onto a sandy track under trees. After $^{1}/_{4}$ mile take the left fork, finally going steeply downhill, with a precipitous drop to the river on the left, exiting onto a road.

7. Turn left over a 'Weak Bridge', following the road for 500 yards to a T junction. Cross over to a bridleway and follow this for $^{1}/_{2}$ mile, winding through trees to another road. Cross the road onto a stony bridleway and farm track leading to Tilford Reeds, turn a corner to the left, and follow the now sandy bridleway, soon leading through woodland, Tankersford Common. After about a mile reach Pierrepont Home Farm and follow the bridleway sign through the farmyard ahead, turning left past the farmhouse and right between fields to a wooden footbridge over the river. This is once more the river Wey, south branch, where pretty water plants can be seen in the clear water. On the left side of the bridge is a ford, shallower than the one at Tilford, for use by horse-riders. This use can mean that the track on the far side of the bridge is often rather muddy, but there are usually branches laid across to aid the walker. After about 100 yards turn left at a junction onto a wide track to the Toilets on the left.

8 [5]. Continue forward, crossing a wide track, bridleway 522, and then bear right after a few yards to reach a road with the car park opposite and to the right. Enter the car park through steel rails and keeping left of a large oak tree, go forward up a slight grassy slope to a track. Ignore the path ahead through trees and turn left, taking the track alongside a fence down to the edge of Frensham Little Pond. With this on the left, follow the track along the sandy edge of the pond. At the end of the pond, with bushes on the left, keep directly ahead on a path leading uphill, soon crossing a bridleway marked with short posts and signs saying 'No Horses No Cycles'. Continue uphill to a junction at the top of about five tracks. Go forward to the edge of the drop and turn left onto a sandy track through gorse leading along the top of the ridge. This high point is Kings Ridge, with splendid views back to Frensham Little Pond, and of Frensham Great Pond lying below on the right.

9. After about 100 yards, exit to a clearing where about six tracks meet. Ignoring a path on the right going downhill to the road, go forward through a horse barrier on a footpath through gorse and then heather, leading along the right side of a sandy bridleway. After about 200 yards turn right and follow the footpath going steeply downhill to a bus stop on the road, A287 to Farnham. Cross over the road and follow the path ahead and slightly left between fences, around the north side of the Great Pond, to return to the car park at the beginning of the walk.

16 Liphook – Folly Pond – Milland – Wardley Moor

Barrie and Margaret's walk

Length: 11 miles or 5 miles by omitting sections 4 - 8. There are no stiles on the shorter version.

Maps: OS Landranger 186, Explorer 133.

Start: GR 842310 Liphook railway station car park.

Transport: South West train services to Liphook. Stagecoach Hampshire & Surrey buses Haslemere - Alton; Hindhead - Petersfield via Liphook; Farnham - Liphook.

Refreshments: Black Fox PH, Liphook on B2070; Rising Sun PH, Milland.

Introduction: The woodland areas on this walk contain a great variety of trees, making this a beautiful autumn walk. Alternatively it can be enjoyed in springtime when the wild rhododendrons are in bloom. The route follows part of the Sussex Border Path.

47

THE WALK

From the railway station walk ahead through the shops to the main road, the former A3 now B2070. Turn left along the road, signed towards Portsmouth and Petersfield, and cross over at the Links Hotel. Immediately beyond the hotel take a bridleway parallel with the road and follow it through to a metalled road. Turn right, through gates marked 'Private No Parking' and follow the road to a lily pond, beside which stands an imposing statue of Lord Strathnairn. He was Commander in Chief, India, from 1861 - 1865. His statue was brought from London and re-erected on 24th January 1965, the day Sir Winston Churchill died.

2. Turn right through gates marked Foley Estate. Continue on the road and shortly pass a pond on the right. Go round the S bend and bear right at a fork to pass farm buildings and a footpath on the right. At Foley Hatch leave the road, keep ahead for 25 yards then turn left at the first fingerpost onto a bridleway. Walk through the wood keeping to a fence-line on the left. Join a path as it merges from the right and continue ahead to a crossing path and a cottage. Keep ahead and shortly pass a second cottage. Immediately beyond a third cottage fork left and gently descend through the wood, bearing left to a T junction. Turn left along a path which eventually leaves the wood at the road to Forest Mere.

3. Turn left along the road passing Folly Pond on the right. This is an excellent place to linger and watch the wading birds, having walked a little over 2 miles. Where the road turns away from the pond, bear right along a bridleway parallel with the road. Reach a further road and turn right. Reach a crossing path and turn left onto the Sussex Border Path [SBP]. After 20 yards bear right [SBP] to skirt the edge of a wood, with open fields on the right. Keep right at a fork [SBP] and shortly pass stables and horse trial grounds on the left, still with open fields on the right. Pass under a railway bridge and turn left between fields [SBP] to a T junction. Turn right and gently ascend to a waymarked post.

Shorter version - Continue for approximately 4 yards then turn left. Although not waymarked as such this is still the SBP. Keep ahead at a private, crossing drive and soon reach the main road [B2070] and the Black Fox PH. Turn left to the junction then bear right towards Milland. Cross a road and continue along the SBP. The track shortly bisects a golf course; watch out for low flying golf balls! On reaching a crossing with a private drive on the right, continue from section 9, keeping ahead on the SBP.

4. From the post bear right for approximately 4 yards to a crossing path. Keep ahead, slightly ascending, and in 50 yards pass another waymarked post. Continue across Chapel Common towards a plantation of Scots pine. Turn left at a waymarked post to go through woodland and heather. Maintain the same direction across the common until reaching the main road [B2070]. Cross over into the road signposted Milland Parish Church.

This is the 3^1/$_2$ mile point. There is seating in the churchyard. Milland church was built between 1870 - 1880 at a cost of £4000. It stands on high ground about 400 feet above sea level. When first built it would have been an outstanding landmark on the county border. Behind the church is the older chapel, probably dating back to the 11th century.

Enter the church grounds, continuing past the church to the chapel, opposite which is a noticeboard explaining its history and present restoration. Pass through a fence-opening beside the noticeboard and go diagonally left to enter a wood. Continue on a broad path and soon reach a crossing path. Keep ahead on a narrower path to reach a flight of 76 steps. Descend the steps, cross a path and continue the steep descent. Turn left towards a house on the right and follow the path down past the side of the house.

5. Reach a stable workshop and turn sharp right onto a grassy path in front of the house. Continue along the edge of a wood with fields and good views on the left. Leave the wood by a gate ahead into a field. Keep to the top of the field to a further gate marked Private Estate. Descend diagonally left to the lower path, pass a pond on the left then ascend to a gate on the left. Go through the gate into a field. Cross diagonally right to a metal gate into a wood. Continue alongside a fence on the right, turn right then left to Combeland Farm. Pass the farm and continue along a concrete sleeper track to Canhouse Lane. Turn left along the lane to reach a railed bridge. At the end of the rails turn left over a stile into a field. Follow the stream on the left for 150 yards then turn right, through a gap in a hedge, into a field. Follow the lefthand boundary to a stile and footbridge into a wood. The path meanders through this beautiful bluebell wood to a stile into a field. Turn left along the field edge to a stile. Cross onto a track and turn right. Pass a house and continue ahead through two consecutive metal gates. On reaching the driveway of Great Trippets Farm turn right to the road.

6. Turn right for 400 yards. Turn left towards New Barn Farm. Keep ahead past all the farm buildings to the end of the road. Turn right then left between fields. On reaching Kingsmead House at Cook's Pond Road turn left for about 80 yards. Turn right on a gravelled track; there's a boulder here marked Pinchers, also a Hydrant sign. At the end of the track cross a stile into a field. Follow the righthand hedgerow until reaching a fingerpost by an opening in the hedge. Here turn left across the field to a gate. Pass through the gate and in 25 yards cross a footbridge into a field. Bear diagonally right to the brow of the field and head towards a fingerpost which can be seen from the brow. Cross a footbridge and go through a gate into a field. Head for the lower gate in this field. Go through the gate and bear slightly right for about 100 yards. Turn right and ascend to a pair of metal gates into Waldergrove Farm. Pass through the farmyard and follow the drive to Milland Road.

7. Turn left for 30 yards. [This is the 7 mile stage. If you continue a further 200 yards down the road to The Rising Sun PH, you must return to this 30 yard point.] Cross over to a gate marked Myers, with a stile beside it. Pass through the gate and turn immediately right over a stile into a field. Cross diagonally towards the right of a lone cottage. Cross two stiles with a plank footbrige between. Follow a lefthand field boundary to a stile. Over the stile cross two more fields, with a stile and footbridge between. Cross a stile then continue with a field boundary on the left to reach a stile by a gate, noting the view to the right of Titty Hill and Telegraph Hill. Over the stile bear left across a wide grassy track to a stile into a field and head towards a stile on the left of farm buildings. Cross the stile, turn left, then cross two further stiles in order to walk through fields, keeping parallel to the drive at Alfords Farm. Do not walk down the drive! On reaching the road turn left. Reach a junction and turn right towards Wardley. Pass Hollycombe School and continue on the lane. Pass a bridleway left then Wardley Cottages on the right to reach a metal gate. Pass through an opening on the right of the gate and continue on a grassy path between fields and light woodland to the road. Turn left along the road. Immediately beyond the elbow turn left onto a farm track leading to Home Farm.

8. At a barn turn left along a bridleway between fields. Pass Wardley Cottage and continue round to a T junction at The Old House. Turn right and climb gently to Robins Cottage. Take a right fork onto a bridleway for a steady ascent through a wood. The path first curves right then crosses a path and continues between hedges to a crossing track. Keep ahead until reaching a drive at Hatch House. Turn left down the drive.

9. At the end of the drive turn right onto the SBP. After 3/4 mile, where the path forks, bear left [still on the SBP but at the time of going to press not marked as such] for 200 yards to emerge at the main road. Turn left along the road to the footbridge and enter the station car park by the steps.

17 Haslemere – Grayswood – Chiddingfold – Frillinghurst

Richard's Walk

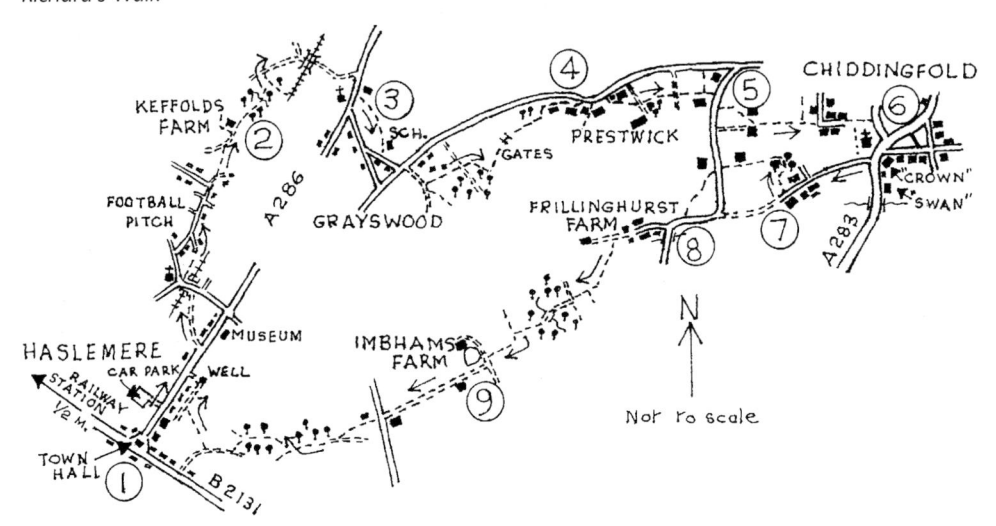

Length: 9 1/2 miles.

Maps: OS Landranger 186, Explorer 133.

Start: *Either* GR 905328 Haslemere Town Hall [start at 1] [Haslemere's main car park is on the west side of the High Street and the entrance is close to the Town Hall]; *or* GR 918348 Grayswood Village Hall car park [start at 3]; *or* GR 962354 Chiddingfold, parking on side road alongside the green [start at 6].

Transport: Frequent South West Trains service to Haslemere station, 1/2 mile west of Town Hall, from Waterloo via Woking and Guildford; or Portsmouth via Petersfield and Havant [hourly on winter Sunday mornings]. Daily Virgin rail services from Blackpool, Preston, Liverpool, Crewe, Birmingham and Reading. Stagecoach bus services Guildford - Haslemere via Godalming & Chiddingfold; Chichester - Haslemere via Midhurst; Aldershot - Haslemere via Farnham.

Refreshments: The White Horse or The Swan PHs, Haslemere; The Wheatsheaf PH, Grayswood; The Crown Inn or The Swan PH, Chiddingfold.

Introduction: This walk passes through a variety of scenery, mainly woods and fields, amongst the gently undulating country between the wooded heights of Hindhead [895 feet] and Black Down [918 feet]. Fine views of these two hills are encountered during the walk. The walk is also of considerable historical interest; Prestwick was recorded as Prestewic in the thirteenth century, Chiddingfold was a centre of the glass making industry from medieval times until the seventeenth century, while Imbhams Farm was an important site for the iron industry which flourished in the Weald before it's decline in the eighteenth century. The route from Chiddingfold to Haslemere follows in part the 'Priest's Path', a modern name that recollects an ancient path and the fact that Chiddingfold was the Mother Church of Haslemere until the mid nineteenth century.

At Upper Sydenhurst [sections 6 & 7] and on the final stretch back to Haslemere across National Trust fields, the route uses 'permissive' paths. These may be closed to walkers without prior notice, in which case watch for local signs and noticeboards.

THE WALK

1. From Haslemere Town Hall follow the High Street using the pavement on the left [W] side. In 250 yards [50 yards before the museum on the right] turn left along a path between buildings signposted 'public footpath to Church Lane' and 'Greensand Way footpath Haslemere to Limpsfield 55 miles'. In 70 yards bend right with the path, still with the brick wall on the right, and keep forward to a road, Church Lane. Turn left across a railway bridge then immediately turn right along a footpath. At the end of this path keep left along a housing estate access road and in 30 yards turn right along another road with a football pitch on your left. Keep forward with this road for 500 yards and where the housing estate road bends left into Whitfield Road, again keep forward. In 50 yards, where the road bears right over a speed hump, keep ahead along a narrow footpath entering a wood. Go straight ahead ignoring turnings on the left. In 450 yards this path is joined by a footpath from the left; here bear right. In 150 yards go forward through an iron gate and in another 60 yards through another iron gate, to reach Keffolds Farmhouse.

2. Just before the house turn right through a gate then bear slightly left up the slope and head across a field from which there are superb views of the Surrey Hills. Pass between two oak trees then keep downhill through a wood. At the bottom of the descent cross a plank bridge and go uphill for 50 yards to a gate marked 'private', where you bear left over a stile into a field. Go ahead to cross the next stile and turn right along a track passing corrugated iron farm buildings. In 300 yards, at the entrance to Damson Cottage, turn right under a railway bridge and follow a track to a road where you turn right into Grayswood.

3. At the first gate to Grayswood Church, cross the road and village green heading towards the school and keeping the impressive modern village hall on your left, to pass between the school and the children's playground. On reaching a road at the Grayswood Common National Trust sign turn left along the road. In 350 yards, at the end of this road, cross Prestwick Lane and follow a bridleway opposite. In 200 yards, on reaching the gates to a sewage works, turn left onto a footpath, ignoring a bridleway going down beside woodland, and keeping between garden fences [NE]. In 300 yards cross a track and go over a stile ahead into a field then follow a fence on your right. In 150 yards enter the next field and immediately turn left uphill keeping a fence on your left. At the top, where there are notable views of Hindhead to the left and of Black Down to the rear right, go forward through two metal gates and continue in this direction, crossing two stiles, for 400 yards. On approaching a farmhouse with a shed in front of it, branch left, keeping a fence and the shed on your right, to reach a road. At the road turn right passing Damson Cottage.

4. Follow the road north-east, passing various Prestwick Farm buildings, for 250 yards where, just before reaching a cottage on the right, you turn right, away from the road, and go over a stile on the right into a field. Keep the cottage fence on your left at first and walk diagonally [ENE] across the field and cross the next stile and a track. Continue forward over another stile into the next field to follow a hedge on your right. At the end of this field cross a stile and continue in the same direction across a field. Go through metal gates into the next field and continue straight ahead to cross two stiles and a track into another field. Continuing in the same direction cross it to a metal kissing gate by three oak trees [to the left of a farmyard with corrugated asbestos buildings in it], pass through the gate to leave the field and continue along a path for 200 yards to a road.

5. Turn right, pass the entrance to Langhurst Manor on the right, and in 50 yards turn left and cross a stile into a field. Keep forward [E] with a line of trees on your left and in 200 yards, with a prominent red brick house ahead, bear right with the path to cross a stile and immediately go forward across the entrance to the house, which is now on your left. Then, keeping a fence on your right and passing the house's wooden garage on your left, bear left and continue [E] with a laurel hedge on the right. Go through an iron gate and cross a stile into the next field then follow a path bearing right [SE] across it. After the right angle in the fence on your left, bear left alongside the hedge, your direction now being east. At the far [NE] corner of the field go over a double stile to walk between high wooden fences. In 200 yards continue in the same direction along a residential road with hedged gardens on either side. At the end keep forward through another iron gate and descend with a path to a cemetery. Keep straight ahead along a track to a road and turn right into Chiddingfold.

6. From Chiddingfold Church lychgate follow the pavement on the same [W] side of the main road downhill [S] for 25 yards and turn right along Mill Lane. Follow this quiet road westwards for 1/2 mile to pass Ukrainian Home, Sydenhurst on the left and reach the tile hung Upper Sydenhurst, with a laurel hedge on the trackside, on the same side.

7. Here turn right across a stile on the left of a metal gate, onto a permissive path following the righthand edge of a field. In 150 yards cross the next stile, still with the fence on your right, and in 100 yards cross a stile on your right into a wood. In 30 yards turn left onto a broader path. In 200 yards go left over a stile and enter a field, keeping a fence on your right. Your direction is now west. In 400 yards pass a house on your right then go straight ahead across the field towards a half-timbered house. Go over a stile, cross a road and another stile opposite, then, bearing left, cross a field [S]. In 200 yards cross two stiles and continue in the same direction to the far corner of a field. Here cross a stile to enter a wood and descend to a road. Turn right.

8. In another 150 yards bear right along a track leading to Frillinghurst Mill, Old Manor and Farm. Pass through the farm and after the last buildings on the right [large corrugated barns] go along a concrete road for just 15 yards, then go left over a stile into a field and cross it diagonally [SSW]. Cross the next stile and keep forward to the edge of a wood where you turn right keeping the fence on your left. Ignore the first stile on the left and continue to the corner of the field where you cross a stile into the wood. Continue ahead ignoring the first track on the right and go downhill to cross a footbridge and then uphill. Continue with this path until you come to a field. Go through a gate with a stile to the right of it and continue forward along a headland path with a hedge on your left. In 250 yards go through a gateway on your left and immediately turn right, keeping the hedge on the right, to reach the pond seen ahead. Turn left and immediately right so that the pond is now on your right and you look across it to the historic Imbhams Farm.

9. Continue along this metalled track with modern farm buildings on your left beyond which a fine view of Black Down comes into sight across the fields. When the track reaches the public road at The White House, cross the road diagonally left and go through a kissing gate to continue south-west along a grassy footpath. Cross over the next stile and turn right along a track to enter the National Trust's Swan Barn Farm. Walk through three fields keeping the fence on your right to enter Witley Copse and Mariners Rewe, also National Trust. In 200 yards bear right keeping a fence on your right [i.e. away from the Right of Way] and in 50 yards cross a footbridge and bear left, continuing west in the wood. In 250 yards, where you see the back of a sign and a seat ahead and the main path bends right, bear left down the slope to cross a stream and enter a field. Bear right uphill to the next kissing gate. Go through it and turn right along a track for 100 yards to where it rounds to the left. Here turn right through another kissing gate and cross a field following a waymarked National Trust [NT] path. At the end of the field go through yet another kissing gate and turn right along a terrace path with views back across the fields. Shortly, at the Haslemere town well, keep left to regain Haslemere High Street, turning left along it back to the Town Hall.

18 Blackdown – Henley – Fernhurst

John and Christine's walk

Length: 12 miles.

Maps: OS Landranger 186: Explorer 133.

Start: GR 921309 Tennyson's Lane NT main roadside car park. Leave Haslemere on B2131 going east and turn right up Haste Hill. Continue uphill over crossroads and Tennyson's Lane is next turning left. Car park is one mile along on the right.

Transport: Stagecoach buses between Midhurst and Haslemere to Fernhurst on A286. From the crossroads walk past the church and cemetery to the small green with the Red Lion PH and recreation ground opposite, and follow directions from 7.

Refreshments: Duke of Cumberland PH, Henley; Red Lion PH, Fernhurst.

Introduction: This walk provides superb views over the Sussex Weald. Blackdown House is passed en route and the Duke of Cumberland pub at Henley makes an excellent pub stop with an attractive garden.

THE WALK

1. Walk along the well maintained track heading south past an open area where there is a box for contributions to the National Trust as well as some information on the area. Continue south along the path for 150 yards, then leave it to the left for a very brief detour to see the beautiful view over the Weald. Northchapel is seen with it's church and on a clear day, to the south-east, Chanctonbury Ring on the South Downs. Return to the path. Walk on for 100 yards and take a left fork. Continue keeping left along this bridleway for 800 yards and after passing a staircase on the left take a bridleway on the right. Continue on past the next signpost but just before a further signpost take a track off left to a viewpoint called The Temple of the Winds. The outstanding panorama at the Temple is from the highest point in Sussex [917 feet]. Blackdown was given to the NT in 1944 by the Hunter family and is commemorated by the stone seat and orientation table.

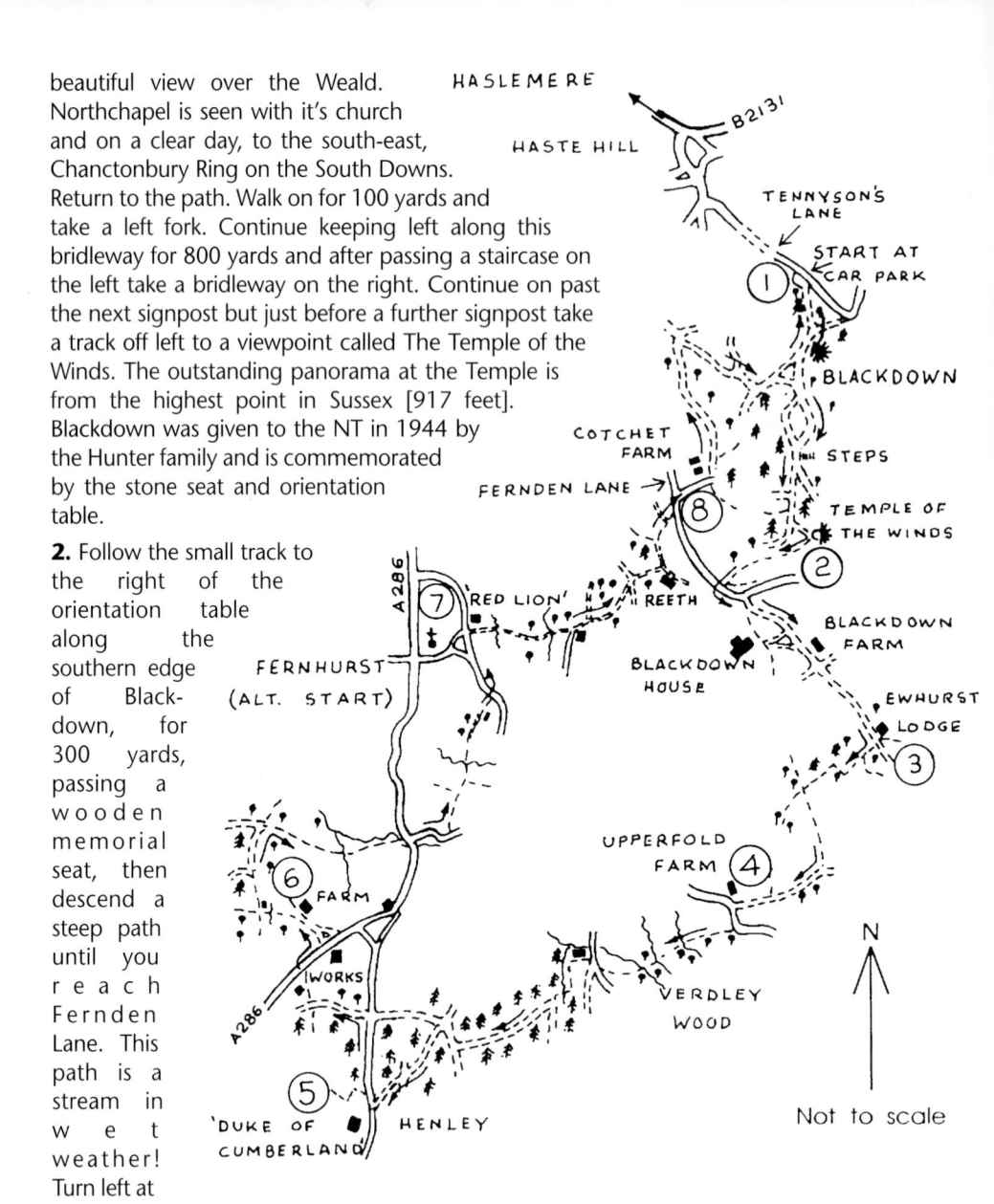

2. Follow the small track to the right of the orientation table along the southern edge of Blackdown, for 300 yards, passing a wooden memorial seat, then descend a steep path until you reach Fernden Lane. This path is a stream in wet weather! Turn left at the road, walk for 300 yards and turn right into a stone gateway marked 'Blackdown Park'. Proceed along the footpath which is a metalled road. After 100 yards Blackdown House is seen to the right. Oliver Cromwell stayed here during the seige of Arundel Castle. The house is not open to the public other than on a few special days during the year. There are exceptionally fine views of Sussex but somewhat marred by the ugly Midhurst Beacon for aircraft using Gatwick. Pass through several gates, keeping cottages to your left and attractive duck ponds to the right. The footpath descends slowly for 1/2 mile to a house, Ewhurst Lodge.

3. Immediately after passing the house take a footpath to the right through woods, later turning right and then left, until the corner of a field on the left is reached. Keep along the righthand edge of this field to a small gate on the left then turn left and cross the field towards pylons. Go over a stile and turn right onto a bridleway which is very muddy in wet conditions. Keep to the righthand edge when passing through a field and stay on the bridleway until a road and Upperfold Farm are reached.

4. Turn left and walk for 150 yards before turning right through a gate by an overhead transformer. The footpath is clearly marked by signposts and crosses a small river which eventually joins the River Rother at Selham. Cross a stile and follow a minor road to the right. After 100 yards turn left over another stile immediately before a white painted bridge. Follow a footpath for 200 yards zig zagging over two more stiles. Take a right turn over a small wooden bridge towards a signpost. Follow the signposted footpath along the broad tracks used by forestry vehicles until a junction with a bridleway. Henley Hill looms in the distance. Turn right onto the bridleway and after 100 yards turn left onto another bridleway. Continue for about 600 yards and fork left onto a bridleway until you meet up with a road that passes through the hamlet of Henley. Turn left to the Duke of Cumberland pub for a well earned rest.

5. Turn left out of the pub by the road to the north. Take the second signposted footpath on the left and follow footpath signs for $1/4$ mile until the A286 road is reached. Take care in crossing this busy road then turn right towards Fernhurst. In 150 yards take a footpath to the left clearly marked in the direction of Lassams Farm. Just before the farm take a footpath to the left which runs at an angle to the drive and continues over a bridge. When you reach some cottages on your right go over a stile directly ahead and take a footpath to the right along the edge of the cottages.

6. Continue for $1/2$ mile, with fine views of Blackdown and Marley Heights to the north, until a fourway junction is reached. Take a bridleway to the right over a small bridge and follow this through woods and fields to the A286. Take especial care in crossing the main road again and follow a minor road signposted 'Lurgashall Winery'. After 200 yards take a footpath to the left across a large field which has a stile at the far side. Follow this footpath, which is well signposted, into Fernhurst. Turn left on reaching a minor road, passing the recreation ground on your right [shelter can be obtained here in wet weather under the canopy of the pavilion] to reach the Red Lion pub.

7. Turn right down a footpath just before the Red Lion pub. Continue along this well defined path for $1/2$ mile. Then, at a footpath sign, turn left at a junction with a lane, by cottages, and start the ascent of Blackdown. The going can be heavy in wet conditions. In 50 yards, at a junction, take a right fork, climbing steadily until a house, Reeth Cottage, is reached on the right. Take a bridleway to the left and after 50 yards, at a junction, continue straight ahead until the bridleway meets Fernden Lane.

8. Turn left down Fernden Lane and in 50 yards turn right towards Cotchet Farm. The main source of the River Wey wells out of the ground into a horse trough outside the farm, on the right. Take a bridleway round to the left behind the house. Keeping the farm on your left and ignoring a bridleway leading off right just past the farm, walk for $3/4$ mile. At a fourway junction take the Sussex Border Path to the right and follow the signs for this until you join the path which was the start of the walk. From here it is a short distance to the car park.

19 Fernhurst – Lurgashall – Northchapel

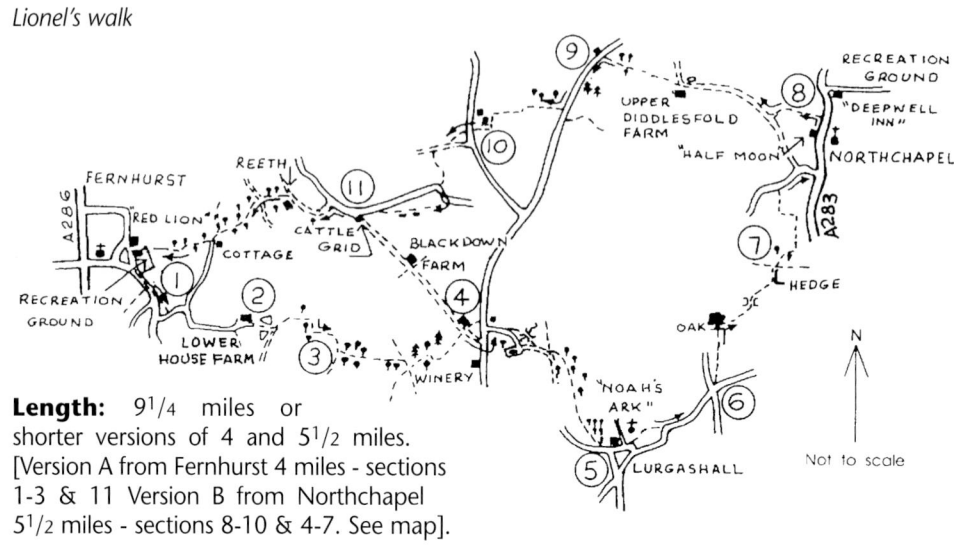

Lionel's walk

Length: 9¼ miles or shorter versions of 4 and 5½ miles. [Version A from Fernhurst 4 miles - sections 1-3 & 11 Version B from Northchapel 5½ miles - sections 8-10 & 4-7. See map].

Maps: OS Landranger 186, Explorer 133.

Start: *Either* GR 900285 Fernhurst recreation ground near the Red Lion PH, via A286 [start at 1]; *or* GR 952295 Northchapel recreation ground on A283 [start at 8].

Transport: Stagecoach buses Midhurst - Haslemere via Fernhurst. From the crossroads walk past the cemetery and the church to the small green with pub and recreation ground opposite. Stagecoach Coastline buses from Petworth to Lurgashall [join at 5] and Northchapel [join at 8].

Refreshments: Noah's Ark PH, Lurgashall; Half Moon PH or Deepwell Inn, Northchapel; Red Lion PH Fernhurst. Tea and coffee are served at Lurgashall Winery.

Introduction: This is a walk through fields and woods, passing snowdrops and rhododendrons in their seasons, with views to the South Downs in clear weather. Blackdown rises impressively to your left on the outward route and you walk its lower slopes on your return. Lurgashall Winery can be visited [including both shorter versions] where a wide range of traditional country wines are available, and in the village itself you can sit outside the pub on a summer's day watching cricket on the green. The descent from Blackdown towards the end of the walk is wet even in summer. Waterproof footwear is needed if you are to complete the walk dryshod.

Lurgashall Winery is open Monday to Saturday 9am - 5pm and Sunday 11am - 5pm, except Christmas, Boxing and New Year's Days. Self-guided Winery tours at weekends. Telephone 01428 707292.

THE WALK

1. From the Red Lion PH at Fernhurst follow the road past the recreation ground on your left to pick up a surfaced footpath which leads between houses and gardens to its junction with a metalled lane. Turn left and follow the lane, past a waymark on the left, through gateposts into a drive leading to Lower House Farm ¼ mile beyond.

2. After passing through a gate into the yard and then directly in front of the house, the path runs between two lakes, bearing left at a fingerpost where a track comes in from the right. After about 100 yards, by a fingerpost, go through a gap into an open field and bear right. Walk parallel with a hedge on your right to a stile and fingerpost. After the first stile look for and climb a second stile on the bank to the left of a gate. The path now bears right with a wood on your right, in a southerly direction, for 100 yards to where a marker post shows the path turns 90° left. This marker post must be watched for as there is no other indication of the change of direction to cross this field.

3. Cross the field to a gap in the hedge, turn right and follow the hedge to a wood. You are aiming for a three-way marker post near the edge of the wood where the path divides. Avoid the path going south along the edge of the wood and cross a stile and wooden sleeper bridge into the wood. Continue through the wood for about 200 yards and at the edge, where the path bears sharp left, go straight on over a small ditch to cross a stile into a field. The ground rises in front of you, between fences, to a gate and stile. Pass a wood on your right to join a track, by a three-way fingerpost, which crosses at right angles at the field edge. Turn right and go over a stile, by the gate facing you, into the wood. After about 100 yards turn left onto a crossing path, keeping the wood on your left. Re-enter the wood ahead and after a further 80 yards turn sharp right before a gate and follow the path round to the left through woodland for 400 yards to meet a drive and a lodge.

Shorter version A. Turn left [see 4 on map] up the drive, passing Blackdown Farm, and rejoin the route at the cattlegrid at the top [11 on map]. Turn left to follow the directions at 11 back to Fernhurst.

4. Turn right on the drive and walk 200 yards to the road. [To visit Lurgashall Winery where country wines may be tasted and bought, go 50 yards down the road on your right. Retrace your steps.] Turn left along the road for 120 yards, then right at a fingerpost, onto a road between a wood and cottages. After 200 yards bear left, leaving the road, and cross a footbridge. Turn left onto a track and follow it for 100 yards, past a caravan site on the right, to a fork beyond a stile on the left into a field. Here leave the track and fork left, climbing over the bank to continue on a path through woods. Leave the woods over a stile into a field and keep along the top edge to cross a series of stiles which lead past an orchard and round to the left of a bungalow to a road. Turn left to the green at Lurgashall.

5. Walk down the road to the left of the green, passing the Noah's Ark pub, and into the churchyard. The path, with the church on your left, drops down to a footbridge then climbs to a road. Turn left on this road and climb 500 yards to a crossroads with a stile and fingerpost opposite on the left.

6. Climb the stile and aim for a large oak tree in the hedge near the top righthand corner of the field. Bear right at a marker post by the tree then, with the hedge on your left, follow it into a dip to a bridge and fingerpost. Cross the bridge and bear slightly right to the lefthand corner of a hedge on the skyline. Continue straight ahead, with the hedge on your right, through a gate in the corner to a waymark post at the corner of the hedge beyond.

7. Go ahead up the field to an isolated stile. You are now at the highest point of the outward leg of the walk. On a clear day you should see the South Downs to your far right and Chanctonbury Ring. Cross the field half right to a stile leading into a wood. The short path through the wood leads to another stile and into a field by a fingerpost. Turn right for 50 yards

57

to a fingerpost by the hedge. Turn left and walk down the field to a stile and fingerpost which you will see half-left in the hedge at the bottom. Climb two stiles and turn left to follow the hedge to a fingerpost at the corner of the field. Turn right and follow the hedge to the bottom of the field and go left over a stile into woodland. Cross two footbridges following the path to a lane. Turn right along the lane and walk down to the main road [A283]. Turn left and walk up through Northchapel to the Half Moon pub.

8. Beyond the pub, at the bus stop, turn left down a path between houses, leading to a field. Follow the edge of the field, with a hedge on your left, for about 200 yards to a gap in the hedge then turn left down a track for 150 yards to a fingerpost at the junction with a farm lane. Turn right and walk up the lane to Upper Diddlesfold Farm 600 yards ahead. Keeping the farm buildings on your left, continue forward by a fingerpost, beyond the lane going off right. Soon go through a gateway on the right into a field. Keep the hedge on your right and aim for a copse and stile 300 yards ahead. Walk through the copse to a road.

9. At the road turn left and follow it for 500 yards to a gateway and stile set back about 15 yards, on your right. Climb the stile and aim for a gateway at the top righthand corner of the field. Go straight ahead through the gate in the direction of a bungalow in the clearing opposite. Go through the gate at the end of the field and turn immediately left, following the path past a mature conifer plantation on the right to a road 200 yards ahead.

10. Cross the road at a fingerpost into a wood and climb 150 yards through trees to a drive. Turn right on the drive and climb a further 250 yards to a fingerpost partly concealed in trees on the left. Turn left onto a footpath to join a road after 250 yards. Turn left downhill for 100 yards then turn right onto a bridleway for 600 yards, passing 'Cobblers' and 'Upper Blackdown', and rejoin the road. Bear left on the road and follow it to a driveway for Blackdown Park, with a cattlegrid on the left.

Shorter version B from Northchapel. Turn left [11 on map] down the driveway, passing Blackdown Farm, to rejoin the route at the lodge [4 on map]. Follow the directions at 4 by continuing 200 yards down the driveway to the road.

11. Continue along the road for a further 240 yards then turn left by a fingerpost and sign for 'Reeth', down a drive which almost immediately bends right and leads to a junction of paths at a house on the left. Take the lefthand path and passing fingerposts, continue downhill through woods. [This is the wet descent warned of in the introduction!] When the path meets a metalled lane at a cottage, turn right into the wood. This path leads back to the recreation ground, car park and the Red Lion pub at Fernhurst.

20 Harting Down – South Downs Way – Compton

Sybil's walk

Length: 8 miles.

Maps: OS Landranger 197; Explorer 120.

Start: GR 790181 Car park at the top of Harting Downs on the B2141, South Harting to Chichester road. From South Harting take B2146 and fork left after 1/2 mile onto B2141. The car park entrance is 3/4 mile on the left, signed Harting Down.

Transport: no public transport.

Refreshments: Coach and Horses PH, Compton.

Introduction: My husband Mike and I enjoyed walking on the Downs and this particular route is associated with warm, summer days. It includes woodlands with wild garlic, bluebells, primroses and violets in their seasons, and open views from the downland sections. The route is not arduous; starting on high ground from Harting Down, it follows parts of the South Downs Way and the Sussex Border Path, with a welcome stop at the pub in Compton.

THE WALK

1. From the car park, walk 50 yards slightly downhill over the grass [N] to the fingerpost on the South Downs Way [SDW]. Turn left and walk to the road [B2141]. Cross the road to the SDW sign and follow the path to, and across, another road [B2146] to a further SDW fingerpost. Walk up the track about 10 yards and turn left. Continue on this wide track for 3/4 mile ignoring all paths to left and right.

2. At a crossing lane with a house on your left, turn left onto the Sussex Border Path. Walk down the lane to Foxcombe House on the left and continue along the track, climbing uphill at first and ignoring a fingerpost on the right where the Sussex Border Path leaves the track. Continue on the bridleway for about 3/4 mile, ignoring paths off to the left, until reaching two six-bar gates at a crossing track. Go through the gates and continue to Hucksholt Farm.

3. Turn right at a footpath sign by an asbestos clad barn and walk up a narrow road. At the brow of the hill ahead there is a view back to Uppark House [NT]. Continue and before the road bends right, cross a stile on the left. Go straight ahead, following the field boundaries to a double stile with a fingerpost, then go across the next field to a lane. Cross the lane, go over a stile and cross a field to a road. Cross the road, climb a stile and follow a footpath sign down the field then bear right to join a track in the hollow for 100 yards to a fingerpost on the left. Climb a stile and walk alongside a hedge to a road. Turn right onto the road and walk 700 yards, using the grass verge, into Compton village. Follow the road through the village to the Coach and Horses PH.

4. Leaving the pub on your right and Village Store on your left, walk up the school access road. Passing the school on your right and the church on your left, go up the path a further

59

50 yards to a marker post. A few yards beyond this turn left. Keep forward, ignoring all side paths, for 3/4 mile to a farm track entrance and fingerpost by a road. The mound on your right is a "long barrow" known as Bevis's Thumb. Cross the road and stile ahead to a track opposite. Follow this for 300 yards, with a hedge on your right and views to Uppark House on the skyline left, to reach a footpath on the right with a marker post.

5. Turn right and walk down the side of a field with a wood on your left. At the end of the field turn right then left through the hedge. Turn left for 10 yards along the field edge to a stile and cross this into another field. Follow the fence climbing gently over two fields to a stile and a fingerpost. Climb the stile, turn left and climb another stile, then walk along the field edge for 150 yards to a fingerpost at the corner of a wood. Here turn half right and cross the field to another fingerpost. Turn left along the edge of a wood climbing further stiles and continue for 700 yards to the corner of a field. Pass a stile in the fence on your right and go ahead to a fingerpost. Bear slightly right along the path with a fence on your right. Follow the path round to the right near a lodge and park gate, with peacocks in the grounds. Continue towards a road but just before reaching it turn left onto a path and walk 50 yards before meeting the road.

6. Cross the road with care to a bridleway opposite. After 20 yards turn left onto a fenced track parallel to the road. When the path enters a wood continue ahead to reach a crossing footpath. Turn right through a kissing gate and, keeping right, go forward 100 yards to a fingerpost, ignoring a path off left with a horseshoe sign on a post. Turn left for 100 yards and at another fingerpost bear left through another kissing gate onto a path with a wire fence on the right. After 400 yards, go over a stile and follow the edge of a wood to a fingerpost by a gate and further kissing gate, with lovely views behind you. Turn left into the wood, crossing another footpath, and follow the path nearly to the road. Then turn right through the wood to walk parallel with the road back to the car park.

21 Didling – Cocking – South Downs Way

Ernst and Ursula's walk

Length: 10 miles.
Maps: OS Landranger 197; Explorer 120.
Start: GR 837185 Didling, south-west of Midhurst, reached by small lanes from either A272 via road to Elsted or from A286 at Cocking. Park on the wide verge south of Woolbeding Farm Ltd., Didling Manor.[Manor Farm on OS Explorer map.]
Transport: Stagecoach Coastline buses Midhurst or Guildford - Chichester via Cocking. Join at 3.
Refreshments: Blue Bell Inn, Cocking.
Introduction: Living on the edge of the county and the Godalming and Haslemere group area, we like going south to the Downs, our favourite area. The attractions of this walk are the superb panoramic views from the top of Didling Hill and Linch Ball on a fine day, orchids on the wayside in season, two old churches and good food in the pub.

THE WALK

1. From the parking spot go to the T junction and turn right to follow a signpost to 'Didling Church'. When the road bends to the right leave it and go straight on into a tarmacadam track with a sign for St. Andrew's Church. St. Andrew's 13th century shepherds' church is on the right. Keep straight on over a stile and through a kissing gate, then uphill over to a stile at the edge of a wood. Climb steeply to a bridleway by a waymark post and steps down in the bank. Here turn left, still going uphill. The opposite bank is a site for orchids. On reaching the top of Didling Hill turn left at a three-way fingerpost onto the South Downs Way [SDW]. After 3/4 mile, ignoring a fingerpost and a waymark post and passing the 'trig' point on the left, turn right at a waymark post onto a bridleway alongside a row of trees, to the woods ahead. Keep straight on past a fir plantation on the left [newly planted 1996]. At the end of the plantation, with a hunters' hide in the corner, turn left onto a bridleway [unmarked at this point]. This bends slightly to the left. Continue, keeping left at a fork and now following bridleway marker posts. On the descent there is the ruin of an old farm hidden in a copse to the left. This point makes a suitable place for a break.

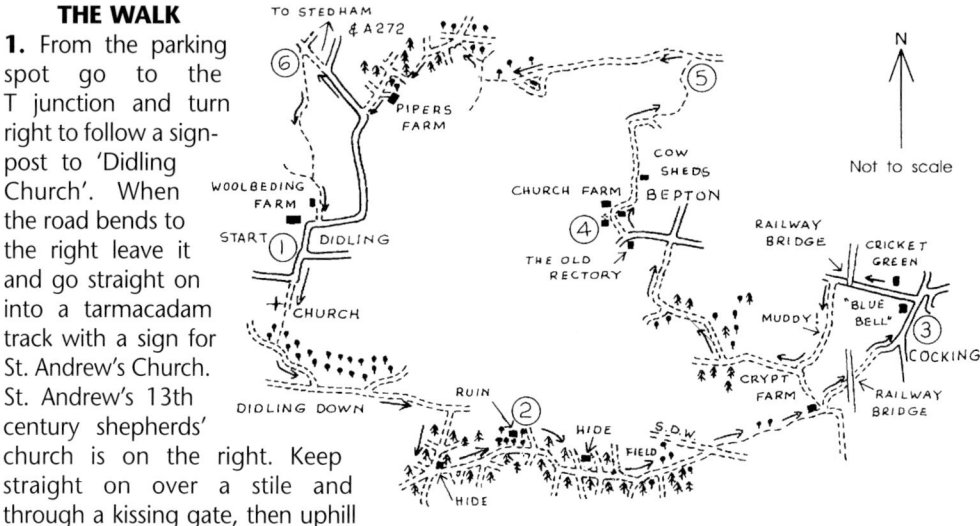

2. Keep going forward and after reaching a hollow, ignoring a crossing path with a fingerpost, the bridleway turns slightly right to the edge of tall trees and then bends half left. Cross over a gravelled forest track by a fingerpost on the left and within 100yards observe a hunters' hide up through trees on the left. At the edge of the woodland, by an obscure three-way fingerpost, join a rutted farm track with fields on your left and keep straight on to a further three-way fingerpost. Bear left, staying on the main path. At the end of an open field on the left, go past a three-way fingerpost and still keep forward through a copse to meet the SDW. Cross over at the fingerpost into a field and go diagonally across this to the next field at a fingerpost. Cross towards the edge of the hedge on the right then follow the boundary to the bottom and go through a copse. Coming out of the copse, pass a cottage on the left and enter Crypt Farm. Go forward along the tarmac road between the farm buildings on the left and right, and at a waymark post turn left along the garden wall with the stream on the right. Pass under an old railway bridge and reach the main road in Cocking. Turn left to the Blue Bell Inn. Time for lunch! [A good picnic spot is beside the cricket green. Turn left into Bell Lane beside the pub and after 200 yards, opposite Old Station House, go up a drive on the right.]

3. Walk up Bell Lane, to the left after the pub, and after passing under a bridge turn left at a fingerpost into a bridleway which can be very muddy. At the top of the rise, at a three-way fingerpost, turn right to follow a semi-sunken lane for 1/2 mile into woodland. At the next waymark post turn right downhill until the track meets a road. Here turn left [there is a road sign to Didling and Harting] continuing past a house on the left and Upper Farm House on the right until you reach The Old Rectory on the left. Beyond this leave the road, turning right to follow a footpath with a sign for the church. Bepton Church on the left is worth a visit.

4. Enter Church Farm and at a fingerpost turn right to pass between the house and the outbuildings. Turn right at a fingerpost and follow the concrete farm road for 100 yards round a lefthand bend to cowsheds on the right. At this point the road changes to a track. Keep to the track, passing a single direction fingerpost on the left, until you reach a waymark post. Turn right and after 100 yards go over planks and a stile on the left into a field. Follow the field boundary on your right to the far right corner of this very large field. Pass into the next field with a stream and hedge on your right. At the end of the field, at a four-way fingerpost, turn left along the field edge with a fence and hedge on your right.

5. Pass into the next field over a stile and plank. Keeping the fence on your right, follow it until a stile on your right leads to the other side of the fence. Cross a plank bridge and go forward at a three-way fingerpost into a wood, then take the righthand track at a fork. When out of the wood turn right at a fingerpost and cross a field to the far hedge. Turn right at a waymark post and follow the boundary and ditch. Turn left at a three-way fingerpost, over a plank bridge, and cross a field into the woods straight ahead. After 150 yards trees give way to brushwood. At a three-way fingerpost turn left and follow a dense wood on your left. Emerging into a meadow, over a stile, go diagonally across it to the far right corner and pass over a stile on your right [ignore a private stile into the farm]. Continue with a barbed wire fence on your left and follow this, turning left and emerging into Pipers Farm. Keep forward to the road and turn right. Follow the road for 300 yards and where it bends sharp right, leave it and go straight ahead into a track at a fingerpost.

6. After 200 yards, at a waymark post, turn left over a stile and follow a path crossing two fields, with a fingerpost at a gap in the trees. Lastly, go diagonally across to a gate at half right, pass through it and bear half left to a fingerpost against the left hedge. With the hedge on your left, follow it until within sight of a farm. Use a stile on your left and pass over to the other side of the fence. At a waymark post keep straight ahead to the garden and cottages on the right of the path. Pass into a road and turn right. After passing the entrance to Didling Manor and Woolbeding Farm Ltd., the starting point is in sight.

22 Midhurst – Ambersham Bridge – Lodsworth – Cowdray Park – Easebourne

Jessie's walk

Length: 9 miles or 7 miles omitting sections 4, 5 and 6 and following instructions from A to C. See sketch map.
Maps: OS Landranger 197; Explorer 133.
Start: *Either* GR 887218 Midhurst Bus Station Town Car Park *or* GR 928231 Lodsworth Village [start at 4].
Transport: Stagecoach buses from Haslemere or Chichester to Midhurst bus station.
Refreshments: The Hollist Arms PH, Lodsworth; The White Horse PH, Easebourne. Midhurst has a café, several tea rooms and a range of pubs.

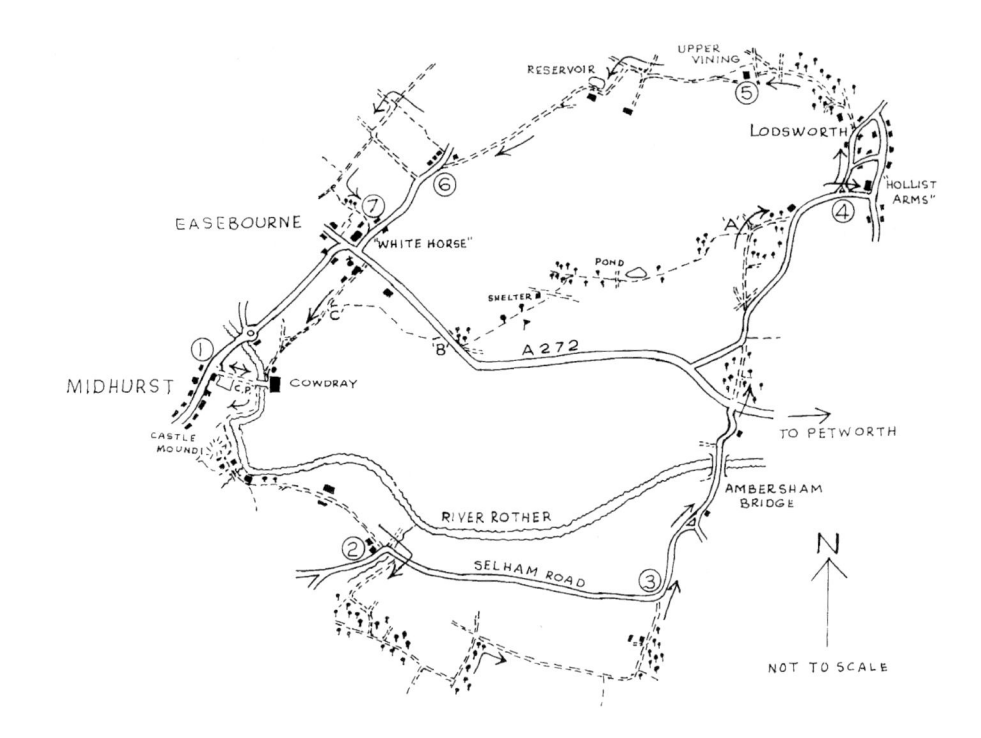

Introduction: I have dedicated this walk to my dog, Jessie, as it is one of the last that we enjoyed together. It is fairly easy going with few stiles, despite being often wet and muddy for the first 500 yards. Take care however, the River Rother can flood and does most years in the Spring following heavy rain! Part of the walk can then be under water, particularly Ambersham Bridge where two feet of flood water in the Winter is not uncommon. The Hollist Arms at Lodsworth and The White Horse at Easebourne are both popular hostelries that do a range of home-cooked food and serve cask beers. Those who are doing the shorter walk may be lucky and find the mobile sandwich bar on the golf course open at weekends: they have been known to serve a mean bacon sandwich! Expect crowds at Cowdray Park during Polo events and as most of the walking is on bridlepaths, take care and be prepared to share them with horseriders. The route includes a 'green lane', crossing the A272 and running, unusually, north/south. This is likely to have been an old route to the coast in the days of Pack Horses - and smugglers. Cowdray Ruins and the Museum are open April - September 1pm - 6pm Monday, Tuesday, Friday, Saturday and Sunday. Admission charge £1.50 adults, 75p children.

THE WALK

1. Leave the car park from the bottom lefthand corner by a kissing gate. Turn right to walk in an easterly direction on the raised causeway for about 400 yards, towards the ruined Cowdray Castle. At the river do not cross the bridge but turn right to follow the riverbank. Keeping to the path, with the river to your left, you pass through a kissing gate and after 100 yards you will see an uphill footpath to your right. [This uphill path leads steeply to the site of the original castle and can be worth the detour. It is possible to rejoin the riverbank by taking a path to your left as you leave the castle grounds.] Continue to follow the riverside path which eventually opens out onto a tarmac turning area between buildings. Turn left, passing a pumping station to your left, and cross a small stone bridge with a bridleway marker post.

63

After a few yards take a bridleway on the left which rises above the river with open fields to your right and trees and bushes to your left. The path gradually levels out on higher ground and continues to follow the river which can occasionally be seen below with commanding views over Cowdray Park and the Polo grounds. After some 500 yards the path leads through a gate and joins a farm track. Keep forward, passing between open fields, to reach farm buildings. Here, beside a gate, still keep straight on between the buildings and follow a metalled lane to join Selham Road.

2. Turn left, passing the gates to Cowdray Park to your left, and shortly turn right on a sandy track [heading south-west] which soon starts to rise with a meandering brook to your right in the valley below. This valley has recently been cleared of massive oaks which were once so common in this part of Sussex. Follow this track as it turns left [east] by a fingerpost and rises with a plantation to your right and then descends, curving right and passing a track coming in from the left. At the bottom of the slope ignore a bridleway going up on the right and keep forward, bearing to the left. As the sandy path rises again ignore a turning off left. There are views south to the Downs where the path levels out and passes between young plantations. [Pass a footpath off right over a stile which leads to the long gone Horsham to Petersfield railway where much of the old civil engineering can still be seen.] Continue straight on past the stile for another 200 yards to a T junction with a bridleway running north/south. Turn left uphill for 300 yards but take care, this is a popular gallop and it is difficult to hear the horses running on the sandy track! At the summit turn right onto another bridleway, heading east, where tree felling has opened up some lovely views. After 500 yards pass a bridleway off right, with a fingerpost, and continue downhill for another 75 yards to where the path turns left. Keep on the main track [north-east] ignoring a footpath to your right. Reach a cottage and keep forward on a metalled track to the right of this for another 250 yards before rejoining the Selham Road at a bend.

3. Bear right along the road. Reach a triangle of roads and keep bearing left. Continue along a lane, crossing the River Rother at Ambersham Bridge. Still following the lane, bear right uphill just after the bridge. Pass a farm to your right after which the lane cuts deeply through the sandstone and at the top reaches a busy road, the A272.

Cross over to follow a 'green lane' opposite, by a fingerpost. After 400 yards this track joins a narrow lane. Ignore a footpath off right. Continue forward up the lane for 200 yards to where a bridleway bears left [north] with the lane bearing off right. Take the bridleway, which is the central grassy path, ignoring a sandy farm track that cuts across the start of the path. At the start there are fields to the left and recently cleared woodland to the right and later woodland either side.

Shorter version. [Point A - see sketch map]. Partway through this woodland [and before the path forks] watch for a fingerpost on the right indicating a narrow, rather overgrown footpath going off left [west]. Turn left onto this and cross a stile. Keep along the righthand edge of a field turning left at the corner alongside woodland on your right. Turn right at the end of the wood and cross a stile. Go diagonally left in the next field across rough pasture. Over the shoulder drop down to a fenced pond, skirting it to the left. Keep forward to a field gate over to your left and go through a small gate at the side of this. Go forward a few feet and bear right on a broad track, but almost immediately bear left off this to keep forward, in line with a fingerpost by the gate, on an indistinct path through the grass. This path goes gently uphill with the ground rising either side. As you near the top of this valley and before reaching trees ahead, watch out for a three-way fingerpost. Turn diagonally left, in line with the fingerpost, going uphill on a small sunken path through the trees to emerge on a golf course. Maintain the same direction, slightly right, to a line of large oaks and a tiled and timber shelter. [There is often a mobile sandwich bar ahead of you.] Keep forward between the oaks and the shelter and come up to a sweet chestnut tree on top of the rise. Continue ahead down the righthand side of the fairway, dropping downhill and passing between two small trees to keep on down to a road, the A272. [Point B on sketch map.]

At the road bear right on the verge alongside the golf course. At the top of the rise turn left across the road to a gate. Go through a kissing gate at the side and turn diagonally right across a field with the ruins of Cowdray Castle clearly visible across the Polo grounds to your left. Bear right by a marker post at the bottom of the slope and reach a stile. Over the stile maintain the same direction towards a bush at the righthand corner of the Polo field. Keep down the side of this with the fence on your left, crossing stiles to reach the playing field entrance. Bear right for a few yards to a T junction with a broad gravel track. Turn left to rejoin the longer route at C [see sketch map] and follow directions partway through section 7.

To continue main route. Stay on the bridleway [north] and after a few yards take a righthand fork which rises into woodland. Continue for 150 yards until it reaches a lane beside stables at Heath End Farm. Bear left along this lane, which leads directly into Lodsworth, for $1/2$ mile and reach a small grass triangle at a road junction.

[**To reach The Hollist Arms pub.** Keep forward downhill, past wrought iron gates on the right and School Lane going off left, for 150 yards to a T junction. Return up the lane to the grassy triangle and turn right along School Lane to rejoin the route.]

4. Turn left along School Lane and after 100 yards fork left, still following School Lane. Soon take a broad track off left, a bridleway, heading into woodland. The track gradually rises, passing drives off left. Follow the main track as it swings left [north-west] and enters a chestnut coppice, ignoring a grassy track which goes forward. Keep to the main broad track through the coppice for about $1/2$ mile, ignoring side paths including a grassy track off left where the main, broad, gravel track swings right. At the end of the coppice come to a junction of broad tracks and keep straight ahead, ignoring turnings to left and right, with splendid views along the Downs to the left. At the next junction of tracks turn right, passing a farmhouse, Upper Vining, on your left.

5. After 20 yards, just beyond the farmhouse, turn left up the bank to a stile and a footpath along the lefthand field edge, which soon joins a track leading from the house. Keep bearing right downhill with, once again, marvellous views left along the line of the South Downs. At the next junction of tracks, by a threeway fingerpost, ignore one going uphill to the right and take the grassy track which keeps forward, leaving the previous track which swings left downhill. After 150 yards turn left, by a fingerpost, down the first field edge with a reservoir to your right in the next field. Towards the bottom of the field the path turns right through the hedgerow, joining a track and continuing past a house on the left. Follow the track round the cottages to where it becomes a metalled lane, descending with views ahead to Easebourne and Midhurst and westwards towards Stedham. Keep downhill, past a turning coming in left, and after $1/2$ mile the lane joins Easebourne Street.

6. Turn right up the lane for 100 yards then turn left, immediately after the third house, onto a track with a fingerpost, leading to farmland. Cross a stile and go ahead over a narrow field to the next stile. Cross this into another field and bear right to gain the old field boundary. Turn left and follow a fence on your left, then keep forward across the field to a stile in the line of trees ahead and descend to a junction of lanes. Turn left downhill. At the bottom, at a junction of tracks where the lane swings left, keep forward on a broad grassy track, soon with open views over Easebourne and across to the Downs again. Continue past a path off right. At the end of the field bear round to the left and shortly go right, over a stile, onto a track running down beside allotments. Continue past a path off right and the cemetery to join a roadway past cottages and houses which leads out to a road, Easebourne Street.

7. Turn right along the road and after 100 yards, having passed The White Horse PH and the local shop, join a main road, the A272. Cross over and turn left, past the church, and after 50 yards turn right onto a wide track into Cowdray Park, with attractive old church buildings on the right. Keep ahead to a gate across the track and go through a small gate to the right of this, continuing beyond Polo pony enclosures on the left. [**C on sketch map.** A fingerpost indicates the footpath by which the **shorter route** comes down beside the polo field and **rejoins the main route**.] Both routes now keep forward along this wide track with the polo field over to the left. The ruins of Cowdray Castle gradually come into sight. Go through a gate and keep forward downhill on a track with a hedge alongside on the right. This bears round to the right and through another gate. Keep forward over a crossing track then bear round left beside a fence and join a surfaced driveway at the entrance to the Cowdray Ruins and the Museum. Bear left along the drive with good views of Cowdray Ruins over to your left. By the large gates, in front of the impressive ruins, turn right and cross a stone bridge over the river. Keep forward along the causeway and return through the kissing gate into the car park.

23 Petworth Park – Upperton – Lurgashall – River Common

John and Christine's walk

Length: 12 miles or 10 miles omitting section 5 to Lurgashall. A shorter version of 6 miles is possible omitting sections 4 to 6. [see map]
Maps: OS Landranger 197: Explorer 133.
Start: GR 967238 Petworth Park North car park [NT] on A283.
Transport: Stagecoach Coastline bus Worthing to Midhurst, via Petworth. Walk 1 1/2 miles north-west through Petworth Park [NT] and start at 2.
Refreshments: Noah's Ark PH, Lurgashall.
Introduction: The walk offers fine views of the South Downs and goes through varied countryside with small rivers, farms and fields which look beautiful with their summer crops. Lurgashall is a quiet, very picturesque village set around a large green with a cricket pitch.

THE WALK

1. Leave the car park and head through the trees in a westerly direction towards higher ground. After 200 yards pick up a broad grass track and keep the northern Park wall about

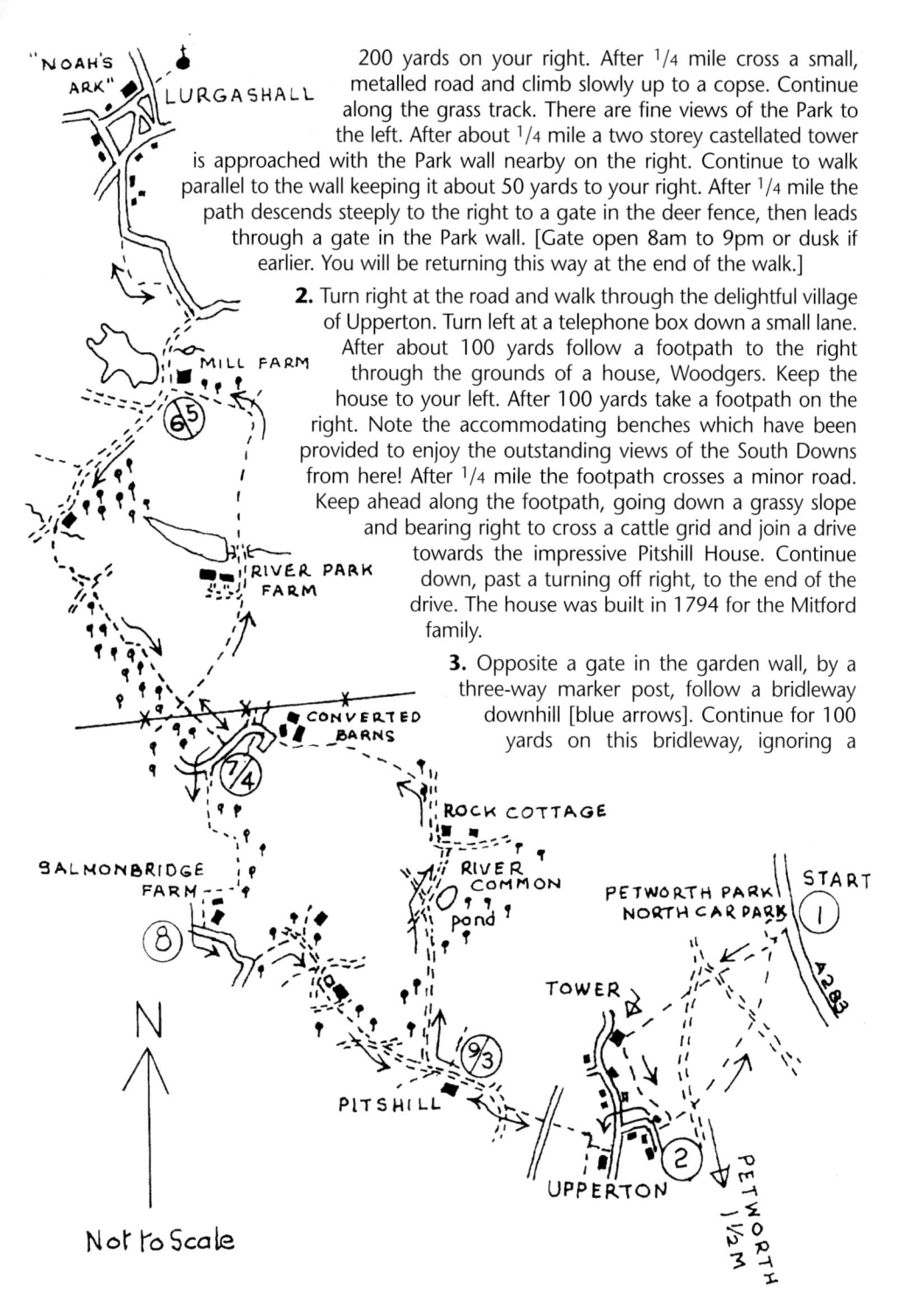

200 yards on your right. After $1/4$ mile cross a small, metalled road and climb slowly up to a copse. Continue along the grass track. There are fine views of the Park to the left. After about $1/4$ mile a two storey castellated tower is approached with the Park wall nearby on the right. Continue to walk parallel to the wall keeping it about 50 yards to your right. After $1/4$ mile the path descends steeply to the right to a gate in the deer fence, then leads through a gate in the Park wall. [Gate open 8am to 9pm or dusk if earlier. You will be returning this way at the end of the walk.]

2. Turn right at the road and walk through the delightful village of Upperton. Turn left at a telephone box down a small lane. After about 100 yards follow a footpath to the right through the grounds of a house, Woodgers. Keep the house to your left. After 100 yards take a footpath on the right. Note the accommodating benches which have been provided to enjoy the outstanding views of the South Downs from here! After $1/4$ mile the footpath crosses a minor road. Keep ahead along the footpath, going down a grassy slope and bearing right to cross a cattle grid and join a drive towards the impressive Pitshill House. Continue down, past a turning off right, to the end of the drive. The house was built in 1794 for the Mitford family.

3. Opposite a gate in the garden wall, by a three-way marker post, follow a bridleway downhill [blue arrows]. Continue for 100 yards on this bridleway, ignoring a footpath off left, then watch for, and follow, a path branching right with a three-way fingerpost rather hidden in the fork of the paths. Keep going downhill on this path, following fingerposts and avoiding sidepaths. At a junction of broad gravelled tracks at River Common, by a four-way fingerpost, take a partly metalled track to the right, passing a pond on the right. Pass the drives to houses on the left and at a three-way junction with a broad crossing track take a bridleway to the left, passing Rock Cottage on your right. Walk for 300 yards, cross a stile on the left and take a footpath through two fields, passing to the left of a restored barn in the second. There are distant views of Blackdown from here. Go through a kissing gate and keep forward down a drive. Cross an old bridge and follow a lane round to the left. In about 50 yards reach a stile on the right.

For shorter version continue along the lane but in about 50 yards, where it swings right uphill, bear left down a track to a field gate. Continue directions at 7.]

4. To complete the full walk turn right over the stile onto a footpath along the edge of a wood. In about 150 yards, at the field corner, reach a four-way junction. Do not cross the stile ahead but turn right along the field edge on a footpath. This goes through open fields to a stile at River Park Farm. Turn right, passing a lake used by anglers on the left. Cross the ford and continue along the path to the right for $1/2$ mile. Cross a stile at a three-way fingerpost and take a footpath to the left to pass through Mill Farm and reach a bridleway. [If you do not wish to visit Lurgashall turn left and continue at 6.]

5. To reach Lurgashall take a bridleway to the right along a minor road. There is a lake to the left used by Fernhurst Angling Club. Continue and, before reaching a road, take a partly hidden footpath to the left. Follow the field edges keeping the hedgerows to your right. After $1/2$ mile reach a footpath to the right. Follow this until a road is reached. Turn left at the road and walk to the village green at Lurgashall. The Noah's Ark pub lies ahead.

The walk returns along the same route as far as Mill Farm. Leave the green at Lurgashall by the road you entered from and take a footpath on the right after about $1/2$ mile. Follow this path and turn left to continue along the edge of a field until you reach a bridleway. Turn right to pass Mill Pond. At Mill Farm continue straight on where, on the outward route, you turned to the right to visit Lurgashall.

6. Continue along the bridleway for just over $1/2$ mile, passing a wood on your left. At the end of the wood turn left at a three-way junction, cross a stile and turn right to follow round the edge of a large field. After $1/4$ mile take a footpath to the right through a gate at a two-way junction. After 50 yards cross a road and then a stile and follow a footpath along the edge of a field with a dense wood to your right. After $1/4$ mile cross another stile at a four-way junction and continue straight on beside the wood, under an overhead power line, for about 150 yards to cross a stile into a lane. [This part of the walk, to the lane, repeats a small section of the outward walk at 4.]

7. Turn right along the lane but in about 50 yards, where it swings right uphill, bear left down a track to a field gate. Keep straight ahead and cross stiles at the far side of this field. Follow the footpath sign, keeping to the left of the next field. Continue round the field edge to find a marker post and turn left with Salmonbridge Farm buildings on the left. Cross a stile and follow a path round to a road.

8. Turn left along the road and go downhill, past the entrance to Salmonbridge Farm. Cross an old bridge and after about 100 yards, where the road swings right uphill, take a footpath to the left through woods. Cross a broad track and bear right uphill. Near the top of the rise, by a marker post where a path joins from the left, keep forward. Continue straight on, past a turning off left, to a T junction with a broad track and a fourway marker post to the right. Turn right along the broad track, passing the marker post and ignoring a path going downhill right. Shortly, turn left uphill by another marker post, on a somewhat overgrown footpath. Pass a house with a tennis court to your left, crossing the drive and keeping forward uphill and into woods. Meet cross tracks, with a marker post to the right, and keep straight ahead. You are now on a bridleway which takes you steadily uphill, past a bridleway coming in left and later a footpath right, to reach Pitshill House.

9. [The walk now returns to the start along the route previously followed - see 3.] Go left along the drive to a cattle grid after which bear left on a footpath up the grassy slope, to a stile and gate. Walk between a hedge and fence to a minor road. Cross the road and follow a path opposite beside a hedge for 300 yards. Turn right at a facing gate and then left at a three-way fingerpost to re-pass Woodgers. Turn left at a small lane and then right at the telephone box in Upperton. [section 2] Follow the road and then go left down the path to the gate into Petworth Park. The return route in the Park can be that which you took at the start of the walk. Alternatively, instead of following the park wall, head directly into the park for 500 yards or so and then walk to the north-east and the car park.

24 Fittleworth – Hesworth Common – Shopham Bridge – Burton Mill Ponds – Fittleworth – Little Bognor – Bedham – Stopham

Monica's walk

Length: 16$^{1}/_{4}$ miles or shorter versions of 7 miles [sections 1 to 7] or 9$^{1}/_{4}$ miles [sections 8 to 14]

Maps: OS Landranger 197; Explorers 121 and 134.

Start: GR 008193 Hesworth Common car park, Fittleworth, at the junction of the B2138 and A283.

Transport: Stagecoach Coastline buses Pulborough to Chichester Wednesdays only along B2138 through Fittleworth. Tillingbourne & Stagecoach Coastline services Storrington, Findon, Worthing and Horsham, Petworth pass Pulborough railway station along the A283. Alight at the church and see sketch map to join either loop of the walk.

Refreshments: The Swan Hotel, Fittleworth; The White Hart PH, Stopham Bridge. Teas served in Pulborough Garden Centre on A283 near Stopham: open 9am to 6pm Monday to Saturday and 10.30am to 4.30pm Sundays.

Introduction: This walk can be done as a complete figure-of-eight or as two separate walks, one to the south-west and one to the north-east of the car park. The walk is in mixed countryside: in open fields, in some ancient woodland, on protected heathland and crosses the Rivers Rother and Arun*. Some road walking is inevitable to reach the bridges across the rivers but all major roads used have pavements or verges to walk on. The walk can be muddy underfoot in parts [e.g. section 10] but much is on light, sandy soil. The open views to the South Downs lift the spirit on even the dullest days. The heathland walked on is protected and unusual birds and flowers may be seen here.

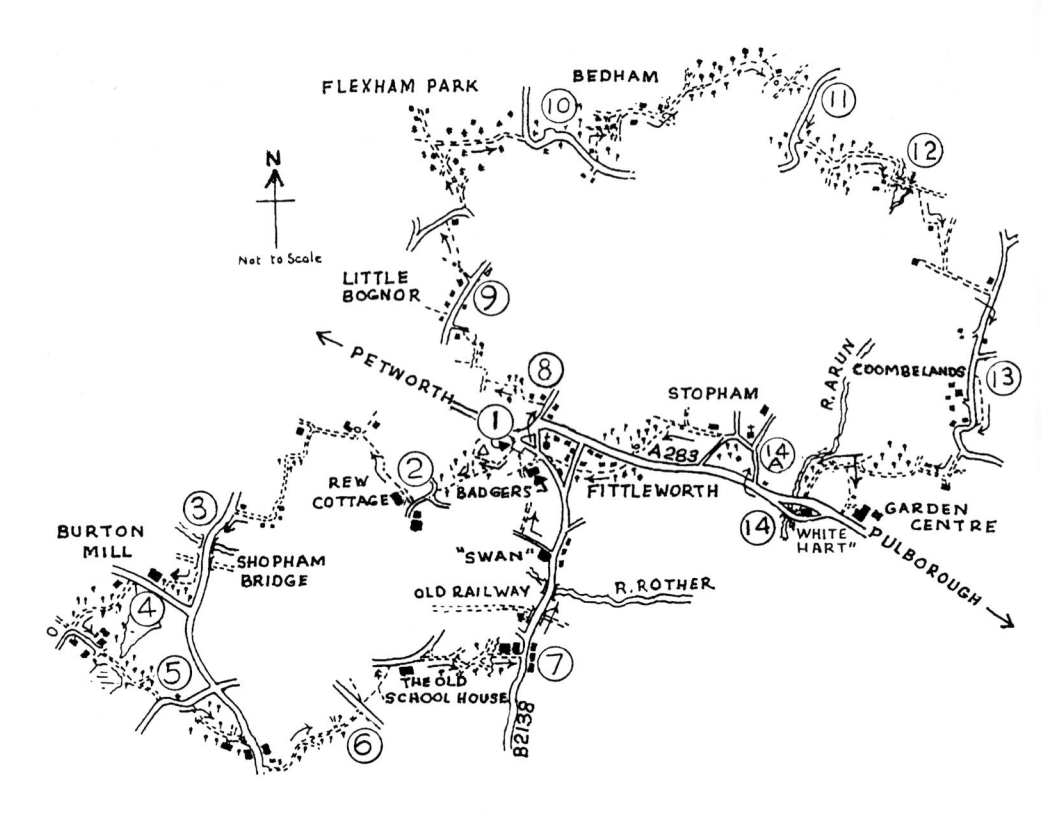

[*Note: after periods of heavy rain the River Arun is liable to flood and a detour, omitting sections 12 and 13 and rejoining partway through 14, may be necessary. This is outlined but OS Explorer sheet 134 would be useful.]

THE WALK

1. Standing with your back to the road take the central footpath immediately behind the green Hesworth Common sign. After about 300 yards through the woods you will reach a sandy path going off steeply uphill to the right. Follow this to the top of the hill where there is a 'trig' point and a seat from which you get an excellent view of the South Downs. In summer the heather and ling in flower is an attractive bonus. Turn left and return downhill by the other obvious path to reach a path junction and a marker post with five yellow arrows. Take a stepped path down to your right [before reaching the seat ahead]. Keep straight on, continuing on the sandy track through woods, crossing one footpath, and keep ahead until you meet a road. Turn left onto the road and go downhill to a T junction at which you must turn right. Walk past 'Two Oaks' and continue a short distance until you reach houses.

2. Just before reaching Hesworth Farm turn right onto a footpath following the walls of Rew Cottage on your lefthand side. After the buildings there are hedgerows on the right and fields on the left with nice views again to the Downs. At the end of the second field go through a clear gap ahead in the boundary hedge, leading over a stream. Immediately after this cross over a stile on your left into another field. Turn right and continue walking with the hedge on your right until you reach a metal gate near houses. Through the gate bear left along a sandy track, with a pretty pond on your right. Go past farm buildings and follow the track through a metal gate and gently uphill, with a most attractive house and garden on your righthand side. Head towards a white painted building at the top of the hill but before reaching this, at a marker post where the track divides, turn left and walk south towards the Downs. Turn right with the track at the bottom of the field, alongside woodland, and then left shortly afterwards, coming out through a strip of woodland into a field with a nice view of the Downs again. Carry straight on down the field towards a farm, Bigenor Farm, directly ahead. At the end of the field you will reach the farm with a nice old wall straight ahead of you. Turn right onto the gravelled farm road in front of the wall and follow this round with the farm buildings on your left. Keep to this until it brings you out to a road. Turn left onto it and follow it across the River Rother at Shopham Bridge.

3. Having crossed the river, carry straight on along the road crossing a bridge over a disused railway. Shortly afterwards, where the road bends gently to the left, you need to go over a stile by a gate on the righthand side. Follow a footpath uphill and parallel to the road. At the end of the field follow the field boundary to the right and walk on with a wood on your lefthand side. There are now good views to the north back towards Fittleworth. At the end of the field is a stile on your left. Cross this, turning into the wood. The path is now quite easy to follow through the woods. Carry straight on along this path with a drop to your right. Eventually the path descends to a road along which you turn right. A few steps bring you to Burton Mill ponds where it is possible to take a break sitting beside the water watching the swans, ducks and other water birds as well as the fishermen. Stop and admire the Mill House down to your right and the view of the Downs.

4. Continue on the road across the end of the pond and take a footpath that goes off on your left along the drive to Burton Mill Lodge. Where the drive swings up to the house on your right, the path keeps forward through a private garden. Follow the path straight on through woodland for some time. It eventually leads to a gate with a private road beyond it and a pond on your righthand side. Turn left onto the road. Once again you have a pleasant view of the Downs and the Burton Park estate. Carry on up the road past a house on the right and keep gently uphill to where there are houses set back on both sides of the road. [Note: the map does not indicate houses on both sides of the road as some are very new.] Take a footpath straight ahead of you. Continue up a slight rise through woods, with water down on your left and the other pond of Burton Mill on your right. Go past this second pond and follow the main path which bears left. Do not go through the gate that lies straight ahead. Fifty yards further down the path the footpath divides. Carry straight on: do

71

not take the lefthand fork. Continue uphill until you reach a gate with a stile on the righthand side. Go over the stile and cross a farm track. Climb another stile immmediately to walk beside a farmhouse, Crouch Farm, and farm buildings on your left. Go through a gate onto a road.

5. Turn left and go downhill following the road. On the righthand side, after 200 yards, there is a bridleway with a sign identifying that you are entering a Sussex Wildlife Trust Nature Reserve. Continue on through the wood beside a fence until you get to a house set back on your right. Keep forward and follow the drive down to your left until you reach a road. Turn right and stay on the road, past a house called 'The Old Poor House', and then continue uphill until you get to a bridleway along a farm track on the left. Follow this track: it bends right past a gate and a house, then soon turns left, going downhill with a wood on the righthand side. At the bottom follow the track round to the left and continue ahead to where a marker post indicates another bridlepath off right. Keep forward along the lefthand track, going along the edge of woodland with fields to your left at first. Walk straight on even when you get to a place where the vehicular track swings off to the left. The path continues forward through open woodlands, with fields again to the left, until it reaches a road.

6. Cross the road and continue straight ahead through the gate opposite. Here there is a Countryside Commission Open Access notice stating that the land you are entering is called Lord's Piece and that there are several tumuli here. The path is a sandy track going uphill towards Scots pine trees, with a pond down to your right. Pass a bridleway fingerpost and as the path narrows into a small gully near the pine trees, look back and admire the view behind you of the South Downs. Continue uphill and keep forward until you reach a gate onto the road. Through the gate turn right past The Old School House. Just afterwards take a bridleway, which continues in the same direction, along a gravelled track on your right. [Not far along the path, but inside the fence on your righthand side, is a notice about heathland management and this might be a good place to watch out for some of the birds that are so special to this sort of country.] Keep straight ahead, past a track coming in from the left, and continue for a further 200 yards to a Y junction of paths. Take the track to the right, following the bridleway and going downhill. Continue down to a T junction and turn left. Go gently downhill and at the next junction, by a signpost and a tree trunk that makes a good seat, keep left on the higher of two paths. [Avoid a path going down to the right.] Keep going straight on, keeping right at the next fork and leaving the vehicle track to follow the narrower, signposted bridlepath over a small stream: do not be tempted to take any of the side tracks. This bridlepath will bring you to Tripp Hill Farm. Carry on through the farm until you reach a road.

7. Turn left onto the road [B2138] and follow it for $1/2$ mile into Fittleworth, first over a bridge across the dismantled railway, noting the station master's house and other former railway houses on the left, and later crossing the River Rother. Use the pavement on one or other side of the road, until you reach The Swan pub on the lefthand side, where refreshments can be taken. Turn left, past the front of the pub, and continue along a lane. Take a signposted footpath on the righthand side which is also the drive to Rotherwood. Continue uphill on the path, which passes to the right of the property, until you reach a gate. Go through the gate and take a footpath diagonally to the left of you, meeting a drive which runs down in front of a house called Badgers on your right. **To complete the 7 mile walk** cross this drive and follow the path opposite back to the car park.

To continue the full route turn right past Badgers and follow the drive down to a road, the B2138. Cross carefully and walk up the road opposite beside the church. You soon reach and need to cross the A283: it is a nasty bend so considerable care is needed. Continue from 8.

To commence the 9 1/4 mile walk from the car park. Standing with your back to the road turn left along a path running parallel with the B2138 road. Reach a junction of paths and turn left down a drive past a house, Badgers, on your right, to a main road, the B2138. Carefully cross this and walk up the road opposite by the church. Soon reach and cross the A283: it is a nasty bend so considerable care is needed.

8. Having crossed the A283 turn right for a few yards then take the minor road on your left, signposted Bedham and Wisborough Green. A few yards down, by the de-restriction sign, take a footpath that goes off left through a gate. Cross a second gate and go over a field, with the walls of Fittleworth House on your right, to cross a stile into another field. Walk diagonally right across this next field to a stile in the far right corner and cross this into a wood. Immediately go over a low fence and walk ahead across the field in front of you, keeping forward past the first oak tree, until you reach a large ditch carrying a stream with a hedge beyond. Turn right and follow the field boundary, soon turning left and shortly right. Still keeping the ditch on your left and ignoring a track across the adjacent field on your left, walk towards the corner of the field. Near the corner you cross a stile on the left and follow a footpath that goes through a wood, still beside the small stream on your lefthand side. Carry on until you come out of the wood, cross a stile into a field and, keeping the hedge on your righthand side, follow the path up beside a house until you reach its drive. Turn left onto the drive and walk down it to a road. Turn right and follow this road into the village of Little Bognor, where there are some attractive old houses. Continue on up the road until you pass a sign on the left for The Grove House and at the end of it's wall take a footpath off to your left.

[However, do stop and admire the garden of the former mill house on the righthand side of the road and, if you can spare the time, stay on the road a little longer to see the mill pond that lies beyond it.]

9. Keep round to the left on a track beside the wall of The Grove House, to a gate. Go through the gate and take the footpath on the right which goes gently uphill. Go through the gate at the top of the slope and over a stile which is only a few yards further on. Cross the field beyond, going straight towards the house you will see ahead of you. At the top of the field do stop and look back at the panorama of the South Downs from Chanctonbury Ring to Cocking Gap. Cross a stile to the left of the house and follow a footpath to a road. Turn right onto the road and follow it downhill and round a lefthand bend until it gets to a very sharp bend to the right. Keep straight ahead here along a surfaced track with a footpath fingerpost on the left. Follow this path and soon bear left by a fingerpost, past a house down to the right. Go straight on gently uphill for some 1/4 mile through the woods of Flexham Park, noting further signs and ignoring the first crossing track. Eventually you will reach a broad crossing track with houses and a road in view ahead of you. Here turn right onto a bridleway going slightly downhill to a gate. Continue straight on. Do not be tempted to deviate to right or left on any of the crossing tracks or paths but continue on the bridleway through coppiced chestnut woodlands. Occasionally, through gaps in the coppicing, you can catch glimpses of the South Downs. You will finally reach a point where the bridleway starts to go downhill, so follow this until you reach a gate and go through this to a road. Turn right onto the road following it around a sharp hairpin bend and uphill to where you will find some fallen tree trunks that might make a useful place for a picnic or drinks stop.

10. Continue to follow the road downhill for about $1/4$ mile and partway down, opposite a farm entrance on the right [Bedham Farm but no sign visible], there is a bridleway as a sharp left turning off the road just before a blue WO concrete marker. Go down this and be surprised to find the ruins of a chapel. [This path is wet even in summer so might not be the best place for a winter walk.] Leaving the chapel on your left continue down to a crossing bridleway and turn right, still going downhill. Keep forward downhill and over a driveway to a metalled roadway. Turn left, following a bridleway fingerpost, past a timbered house on your right. Continue on the roadway past a house on your left and just after this a bridleway sign indicates where you turn to the left. Almost immediately take the righthand fork. Shortly after this you will reach a Sussex Wildlife Trust Information Board with details of The Mens, the area of ancient woodland you are about to enter. At this point take the righthand footpath and follow this through the woodland on a frequently damp and muddy path. Continue on until you reach a gate with a stile beside it. Cross the stile into the open space beyond it, bear right and go through a gate into a wood opposite. Follow a path through the wood, crossing a bridge over a stream. Continue on this path through the wood, bearing hard left, as indicated by a footpath sign, beside a house on your lefthand side. Keep following round to the left past the garage to the house on your left and a pond on your right and walk forward down a clear grassy area. At the end of this grassy area, with a field gate on your left, turn right and continue on through the wood, crossing a long straight footpath, until you reach a road.

11. Turn right along the road. You are now on the route of the Wey South Path which you follow for some time, back towards Pulborough. Follow the road until you reach the zig-zag double bend sign with Round Copse House on your lefthand side. Turn left onto a track with a bridleway sign and continue on this down towards the river, bending sharply round to the left where another bridleway goes off to the right. Keep ahead over a cattle grid, past a drive off left, following a farm lane through open country with a good view of the Toat Monument on the hill ahead, until you come down and swing right towards the bridges that cross the River Arun.

[If the river is flooded you can make a diversion here by walking along the edges of the raised fields on the right to the farmhouse and then turning right uphill along the field edge. Just above the house turn left over a stile in the hedge. Still following the hedge, now on your right, continue to follow footpath signs uphill and around the edge of the next field, curving round to the left. Ignore the first stile on the right and cross one ahead of you into woodland. Follow a twisting path to another stile into a lane. Turn left uphill passing a cottage on the right. Follow the lane, now surfaced, for $1/2$ mile to a cluster of farm buildings. Turn left and then right by the farmhouse and continue along a roadway for about a mile to reach Stopham village, ignoring side paths and passing a road off right by a pond. Continue past the church and turn right at the road junction to re-join the original route at 14A.]

12. There are two bridges to cross: the first an old stone one, the second a modern metal one. Shortly after the second, cross a stile on your right into a field and walk diagonally left across this to the far corner. In this corner is a small footbridge and almost immediately a very high stile which really challenges the knees! Then go through a gate and follow the field boundary, keeping the hedge on your right, until you reach a stile ahead of you at the far end of the field. Cross this stile into a lane and bear right. Follow the lane to a T junction and turn left. Follow a farm lane until you meet a road and turn right. Keep straight on along this narrow road for some distance, initially following it down a dip and then going at first gently, and then more steeply uphill.

13. At the top of the rise, when you reach large gates either side of the road, note the 'Horses galloping - Cross with care' sign and go over a stile on the left by a fingerpost. Walk downhill on a path running parallel to the road. Keep the hedge on your right side, enjoying views of the South Downs and catching a glimpse of Pulborough church away to your left. Continue down, past the entrance to Coombelands opposite, now with a large evergreen hedge on your left. At the bottom of the hill bear right and out through a gate onto the road. Turn left and follow the road which soon bends right and then left uphill. At a further bend left in the road, beside a sign reading 'Caution - race horses on road, please drive with care', take a bridleway on your right along a farm lane that goes straight on up the hill. At the top, with an old barn straight in front of you and before a gate, take a bridleway up the track to your right, passing in front of a house and go through a gate turning left into the woods. Follow this bridleway along the edge of the woods. Eventually, at a marker post where you turn left, you will see the River Arun away down to the right. About 200 yards further on there is a footpath going off on the left over a stile. [If you want to stop for **tea or light refreshments at Pulborough Garden Centre** it is only a short distance along this footpath. Afterwards turn right out of the Garden Centre and walk along the righthand side of the road, crossing over only a short distance further on, to rejoin the rest of the walk at 14, by The White Hart pub.] If not distracted, carry straight on, ignoring a turning right, and continuing forward along the top where the path narrows, until this path goes downhill to a road, the A283.

14. Cross the road to the old stone bridge, with the White Hart pub for meals and refreshments on the left. Turn right to cross the bridge and follow the tarmac path until you reach the main road. Turn left and walk on the pavement as far as the first turning right, signposted Stopham 1/4 mile. Cross the road to walk up to this small village which has an attractive 12th century church. Continue uphill past the War Memorial and the turning on the right to the church. [14A] Follow the road round to the left to a road junction. Turn left down a lane. Almost immediately, where this lane swings left, keep forward along a bridleway past Coronation Cottages. Continue on this through woodlands with fields to your left. Follow a footpath sign straight on when the bridleway bends right and continue as it passes quarries on your right. Watch out for another footpath sign and take a left fork, still with fields to your left. Follow a path through the woods until, immediately before a road, you go down steps and turn right by a marker post to reach a stile by a gate. Cross the road and follow the footpath opposite you across Fittleworth Common, keeping houses on your right and finally going between fences, with gardens either side. Keep forward out to a road. Cross this and walk straight on between more hedges and fences to emerge on the B2138 road beside the church. Cross the main road and retrace your steps up the drive to Badgers, then turn right on the path leading back to the car park.

25 Chantry Post – South Downs Way – Chanctonbury and Cissbury Rings – Findon

Roger and Jill's walk

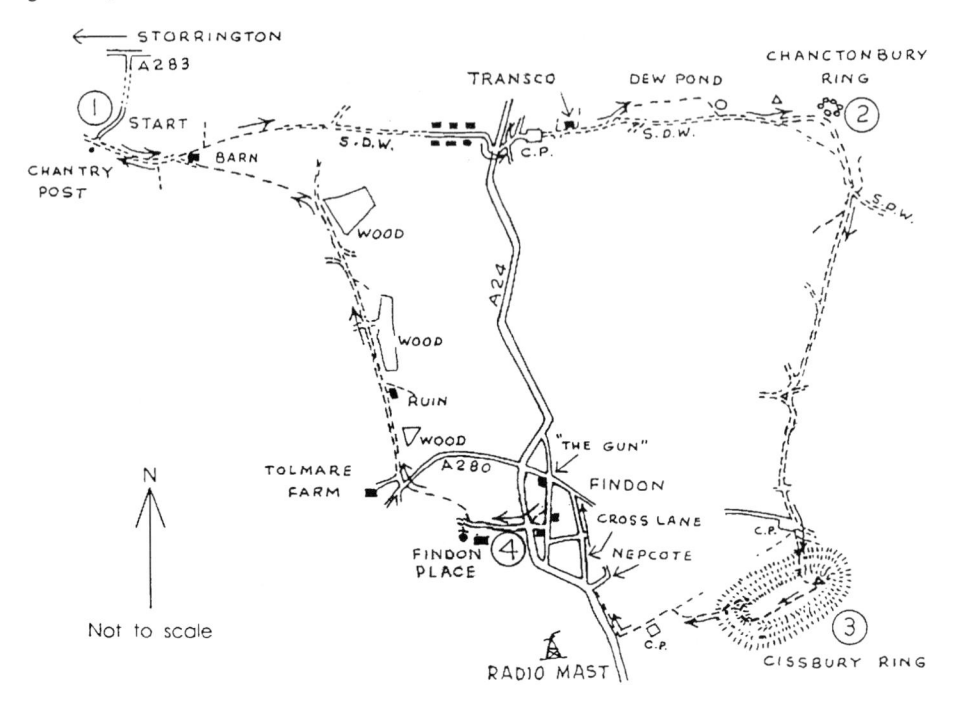

Length: 11³/₄ miles.

Maps: OS Landrangers 197 first and last ¹/₂ mile, 198 remainder of walk; Explorer 121.

Start: OS GR 087119 Chantry Post car park on the South Downs Way. Take the A283 east out of Storrington and the second turning right after the mini-roundabout in the High Street, into Chantry Lane. It is clearly signed 'Downs 1¹/₂ miles' and 'Chantry Trading Estate'. The car park is at the top on the Downs, where the SDW crosses east to west.

Transport: Stagecoach Coastline buses to Storrington or Findon [start at 4].

Refreshments: The Gun Inn, Findon [9 miles]. We suggest you have a coffee stop on Chanctonbury Ring and a picnic lunch on Cissbury Ring.

Introduction: On a good day a fine downland walk passing a well known Sussex Beacon and an Iron Age fortress with stunning views across the Sussex Downs. Chanctonbury Ring is a smaller earthworks than Cissbury upon which a clump of beeches was planted in the 18th century. It's a famous landmark and viewpoint for all Sussex people. Cissbury Ring is an extensive hill fort dating from the late Iron Age, about 200BC. The outer ring is nearly 1¹/₄ miles long and encloses 82 acres. There are many traces of flint mines, all of which have now been filled in, and so many flint implements were found that the area was known as 'the flint Sheffield'. During Roman times the height of the ramparts was raised to increase the fortification of the ring and the Second World War left its mark as the area was used by the army for training. Nowadays the ring is protected by the National Trust.

THE WALK

1. Chantry Post to Chanctonbury Ring - $3^{1}/_{2}$ miles. Turn left from the top of the lane, signed towards Washington, and walk east along the South Downs Way [SDW]. When you breast the first rise you will see Cissbuy Ring to the south east. Follow the SDW taking the left fork and passing a tin barn on your right. Keep ahead on a broad track along the crest of the Downs, later ignoring a path left signed SDW alternative route. The track finally descends and becomes a metalled lane before meeting a main road [A24]. Cross the road and take a tarmac lane leading uphill through a car park. Still following SDW signs continue climbing on a broad track which forks left. Shortly after passing a Transco installation on the left, leave the SDW by taking a bridleway through the gate ahead and to the left of the track. Continue climbing through disused chalk pits towards a fence at the top of the hill. Go through a gate and over the brow of the hill to reach a fence ahead. Turn right and drop down to a gate, skirting a dew pond on your left. Turn left through the gate, rejoining the SDW, with Chanctonbury Ring, or what is left of it after the gales of 1987, ahead of you. This makes a good coffee stop with, on the east side, views of the Devil's Dyke, Brighton and Steyning and to the south Cissbury Ring and the sea.

2. Chanctonbury Ring to Cissbury Ring - $2^{3}/_{4}$ miles. Continue east along the SDW and through a gate with a cattle grid. At a four way junction turn right [south] leaving the SDW for good. Follow the path without deviation, keeping straight ahead over a junction of tracks, to Cissbury Ring. At the foot of the ring walk through a car park and cross a road. Pass through a gate by the National Trust sign for Cissbury Ring and keep ahead to an Information Board. Continue up the hill, bearing right over a broad track, to a kissing gate and steps. Climb a second flight of steps to the top of the inner ring and continue uphill until you see the 'trig' point [602 feet], a concrete pillar, on your left. On a clear day you can see from the Seven Sisters eastwards to the Isle of Wight westwards, from this view point. It's a good place to eat your picnic lunch.

3. Cissbury Ring to Findon - $2^{1}/_{4}$ miles. Turn right, westwards, from the trig point and follow the path along the top for 540 yards, bearing left to reach the inner ring. Climb steps on the right and follow the ring west for 4 to 5 minutes until you see a gate just below the lower ring. Continue on and find steps leading down to go through this gate. Continue diagonally left, westwards, across the hill in line with a radio mast on the hill opposite. At the bottom of the hill pass through a kissing gate and continue down a path between a field and brambles to join a marked footpath. Continue downhill to a grassy area with a car park on the left. Keep beside the hedge on the right and go down beside gardens to a main road, the A24. Turn right along the road and head north towards Findon. Take the second road to the right, Cross Lane, and keep ahead for nearly $^{1}/_{2}$ mile to reach shops and a coffee bar. Beyond this, in the square, is the Gun Inn, dating from 1675. At the Gun Inn turn left along High Street to reach Findon Manor Hotel on the left. Turn right by a fingerpost onto a footpath. Follow this round behind houses and cross a field to emerge beside a gateway on the A24.

4. Findon to the Chantry Post - 3$^{1}/_{4}$ miles. Cross the main road [A24] and go up the drive opposite to Findon Place. Opposite the church turn right through a kissing gate. Follow the footpath, crossing a stile and continuing uphill past Findon cricket ground on your right. Cross the stile to the left at the top of the path and continue uphill going west, pausing to look back across the fields to Chanctonbury and Cissbury Rings and towards the Chantry Post in the north west. Cross a stile and a road [A280]. Take a concrete farm road opposite, past a sign for Tolmare Farm, and continue walking ahead, north, through a gate. Go through several further gates and keep forward, ignoring turnings to left and right, until some 1$^{3}/_{4}$ miles ahead a stand of trees is reached and passed on your right. Turn left at a footpath sign and continue uphill to a gate. Pass through the gate and walk on, past the tin barn on your right, to the starting point of the walk at the Chantry Post.

Notes

Notes